Shed no tear! O shed no tear!

The flower will bloom another year.

Weep no more! O weep no more!

Young buds sleep in the root's white core.

John Keats (1795-1821) England, from *Faery Song*

# The Romantic
## Language of Flowers

# The Romantic Language of Flowers

Gill Davies
Gill Saunders

WORTH PRESS

This book is dedicated to **Peggy Vance** to whom the publisher
gives thanks for all the support in the creation of the book in which
Fanny Robinson's botanical illustrations were first published,
*The Country Flowers of a Victorian Lady* by Apollo Publishing Ltd. in 1999.

First published in 2012 by Worth Press Ltd, Cambridge, England. info@worthpress.co.uk

© Worth Press Ltd, 2012

Text © Gill Davies, Gill Saunders
The authors have asserted their rights under the Copyright, Designs and Patents Act 1988
to be identified as the authors of this work.

This publication contains material based on an original work, "The Book of Memory",
in which John Luscombe and Grant Luscombe are recognised as the copyright holders.
A royalty will go to support the work of Landlife, the charity making new places
where wildlife can flourish for people to enjoy.'

British Library Cataloguing in Publication Data. A catalogue record for this book is available from the British Library

ISBN: 978-1-84931-061-1

10 9 8 7 6 5 4 3 2 1

Consultant Editor: Cristina Galimberti
Design and layout: Arati Devasher, www.aratidevasher.com
Editor: Vivienne Prior
Picture research: Gill Davies

Printed and bound in China

# Contents

# Introduction

This entrancing book explores the Language of Flowers (Lingua Flora) from two directions: the first half draws upon an exquisite nineteenth-century collection of watercolours, *The Book of Memory* by Fanny Robinson, an amateur artist and flower lover (1802–1872). The second section gathers in further flowers and discovers the worldwide impact of flora through history to today.

The Book of Memory was created over a number of years; no one knows precisely when, but Fanny was still at work on her elegant renderings in her forties – if it was to be a keepsake or gift, its intended recipient remains a secret. When Fanny was compiling her book, sketching and painting were very much part of a middle-class girl's accomplishments, with botany considered an 'amusement for the ladies'. Many guides to wildflowers and garden plants were written by – and for – women.

Fanny's paintings encapsulate all the romance of a long-lost era when flowers were an important means of communication in a romance or friendship. Fierce chaperones, familial protection or being in service cast an iron corset on emotional activities, just as the whalebone girdles restricted the waistline! As an aid to sweethearts in their struggle to make their feelings known while not flaunting the strict codes of behaviour – flowers served to carry messages in the most charming way and developed into a minutely codified Language of Flowers.

Symbolic meanings have long been attached to flowers – in religion, heraldry, painting, literature and daily life. The iris and

lily both appear in early paintings of the Virgin Mary as emblems of her purity. From Greek mythology came the association of the narcissus with egotism and the hyacinth with sorrow. Flower meanings permeate folklore, Biblical references and the works of Shakespeare. Red and white roses served as emblems for the warring English during the 1400s Wars of the Roses while medieval gardens were created to reflect the symbolism of flowers – a practice that continued through the Renaissance and religious art.

By the early 1700s, the stage was set for Lady Mary Wortley Montague, the resourceful wife of the British ambassador to Constantinople. She penetrated the royal harem and unveiled the Turkish secret language of flowers. Beautiful blooms had long been romantic tokens in the East but now friends and sweethearts in the West began to send secret messages to each other – mainly through flowers but also grasses, herbs, trees and fruit. *Lingua Flora* developed into a complex language.

Each flower had a specific meaning, dictated by its variety, colour, and placement, with individual flowers, buttonholes, posies or bouquets conveying clear signals. The sender might pay court, reject a suitor, express admiration, friendship, unhappiness or disappointment. Every subtle shade of emotion could be communicated as the precise arrangement (and order) added succinct detail. Flower angles – and whether in the hair or as buttonhole or corsage – carried specific meanings. A bouquet tied with a ribbon to the left indicated that the flowers said something about the sender; a ribbon tied to the right meant that the meaning applied to the recipient. A stem placed upside down implied that the opposite meaning was intended. Removing the thorns said, "Everything to hope for"; removing the leaves meant, "Everything to fear".

All this was at a time when a plethora of flowers also adorned costumes, hats, jewellery, china and home furnishings. As the complexity of symbolism increased, handbooks were written – often published anonymously – including *Le Language des Fleurs* by Charlotte de la Tour in France in 1818. A hugely successful English translation followed in 1834 and multiple titles flowed in their wake, including Kate Greenaway's *Language of Flowers* in 1884. The Reverend Robert Tyas, author of several children's botany books, published "The Sentiment of Flowers"; or, "Language of Flora" in 1842, and "The Handbook of the Language and Sentiment of Flowers" in 1845. Thomas Miller's "The Poetical Language of Flowers," appeared in 1847 and Anna Christian Burke 's "Illustrated Language of flowers" in 1856. Each offered seasonal floral and anecdotal advice to those wishing to send coded messages. If some meanings seem odd it must be remembered that they draw upon original sources in other languages (especially French) wherein their names meant something entirely different! Moreover, prudish English translators lessened any erotic values – for example, reducing the heliotrope's 'ecstasy' to the less potent term 'devotion'.

The Language of Flowers survives, albeit sometimes to an audience unwitting of its particular intricacies and values! The fresh piquancy of the flower studies in this book and the tender sentiments they encapsulate still delight a century and more beyond their creation. May they long continue to do so – both in their own right but also in their encapsulation of bygone times and through the fascinating array of emotions they express so sweetly. From Ottoman traditions, through medieval times, Shakespeare's pen and French romantics onwards, flower symbolism has coloured our lives and inspired artists. Now let us discover more about this heritage. There are fascinating facts about the blooms, the emotions they expressed and their associated traditions. This is an exploration of nature's exuberance – in both the flowers and in our hearts.

# The Romance of Flowers: A Gentle Code

## Pansies & Forget-Me-Nots

THE PANSY and the FORGET-ME-NOT are among the most familiar symbols in the Language of Flowers. Pansies take their name from their French name *pensées* (meaning 'thoughts'). This association had become commonplace by the sixteenth century: in Shakespeare's *Hamlet* the deranged Ophelia runs through a litany of flowers and herbs with symbolic meanings that would have been familiar to many in the audience. She begins, "There's rosemary, that's for remembrance; pray, love, remember: and there is pansies, that's for thoughts."

The symbolism for the forget-me-not is self-evident, but the name seems to have come into English usage quite late, popularized by Coleridge in his poem *The Keepsake* (1802), and inspired by German folktales.

**PANSY**
Latin name *Viola spp.*
Meanings**:** I think of you, merriment, think of me, heart's ease
Habitat*:* Garden
Colours**:** Blue plus many other colours and often with a 'face' pattern
**Fun Facts**
A honeyflower together with a pansy tells the beloved, "I am thinking of our forbidden love."
American pioneers believed that a handful of pansies or violets taken into the farmhouse in spring ensured prosperity.

**FORGET-ME-NOT**
Latin name: *Myosotis sylvatica* comes from the Greek for 'mouse's ear'
Meanings: Faithfulness and enduring true love, memories, don't forget me
Habitat: Wet soils, near lakes and rivers and in shallow water
Colours: Blue, mauve and pink
**Fun Facts**:
A German legend tells how when God named all the plants, one cried out, "Forget-me-not, O Lord!" to which God replied, "That shall be your name."
In the 1400s, it was supposed that the wearers of the flower would not be forgotten by their lovers and it was often worn by ladies as a sign of enduring love.

*Heartsease! One could look for half a day upon this flower, and shape in fancy out full twenty different tales of love and sorrow that gave this gentle name.*
Mary Howitt (1799–1888) England

*The sweet forget-me-nots
That grow for happy lovers*
Alfred Lord Tennyson (1809–1892) England,
from *The Brook*

*Flowers have an expression of countenance... Some seem to smile; some have a sad expression; some are pensive and diffident*
Henry Ward Beecher (1813–1887)
United States of America,
from *Star Papers: A Discourse of Flowers*

# Snowdrops

SNOWDROPS have been favourites in English gardens since Elizabethan times. As they are among the few plants that flower in winter, it is hardly surprising that they have come to represent Hope. For some authors, notably Robert Tyas, they also mean Consolation because they seem to promise that spring is coming and offer us a consoling pleasure towards the end of winter. Indeed, one of the alternative names for the snowdrop is 'snow piercer'.

Latin name: *Galanthus nivalis*
Meanings: A friend in adversity, consolation and hope
Habitat: woodland
Colours: white with green marks

**Fun Facts**

'Moly' the mysterious magical herb in Homer's *Odyssey* – used as an antidote to the poisons of Circe, goddess of magic – may perhaps have been a snowdrop. The plant does contain a substance called galantamine (used to treat Alzheimer's disease) that helps to improve memory.

Legends tell how, when Adam and Eve were expelled from the warm Garden of Eden into winter, an angel transformed some snowflakes into snowdrop flowers, to give hope that the spring would come eventually.

The Latin name *Galanthus* means "milk flower".

The drop in its common name is as in eardrop – an old name for earring.

*The Snowdrop, in purest white array*
*First rears her head on Candlemas day.*
Old folklore rhyme

Chaste snowdrop, venturous harbinger of spring,
And pensive monitor of fleeting years!
William Wordsworth (1770–1850) England,
from *To a Snowdrop*

There it stood, so delicate and so easily broken, and yet
so strong in its young beauty; it stood there in its white
dress with the green stripes
Hans Christian Andersen (1805–1897) Denmark,
from *The Snowdrop*

# Primrose and Wild Strawberry

THE FLOWERS on this page are associated with fond reminiscence and happiness. Most writers on the Language of Flowers agreed that the primrose, traditionally a symbol of spring, represents Early Youth. Its common name comes from the medieval Latin *prima rosa*, the "first rose" of the year and also from the Old French *primerose*.

The strawberry is given the emblematic meaning of Perfect Goodness. In some books the strawberry blossoms themselves have the additional meaning of Foresight. This association between the strawberry and ideas of goodness probably arises from the delicate flavour of the fruit; the berries of the wild plant are much smaller than the cultivated strawberry we eat today, but also much sweeter. One of the many kinds of wild food to be found on a country walk, they were often picked and eaten by children.

## PRIMROSE

Latin name: *Primula vulgaris*

Meanings: early youth, eternal love, I can't live without you, modest worth and silent love
Red ones mean unpatronized merit

Habitat: Open woods and shaded hedgerows

Colours: Pale yellow; occasionally pink

**Fun Facts**

Harbinger of spring, the primrose was the favourite flower of British Prime Minister Benjamin Disraeli.

Its leaves can be used to make tea, and the young flowers are the main ingredient of primrose wine.

Taking the primrose path means the pursuit of pleasure, as referred to by William Shakespeare's Hamlet: "the primrose path of dalliance".

## WILD STRAWBERRY

Latin name: *Fragaria vesca*

Meanings: Perfect goodness, excellence, foresight

Multiple habitats: hillsides, by paths and roads, meadows, young woodlands, and clearings

Colours: White flower and red fruit

**Fun Facts**

Archaeological excavations suggest that wild strawberries have been enjoyed since the Stone Age.

The woodland strawberry was first cultivated in Persia and then its seeds were taken along the Silk Road to Europe.

Helps digestion, removes tartar from teeth and prevents gout.

*Doubtless God could have made a better berry (than
the strawberry), but doubtless God never did.*
William Allen Butler 1825–1902
United States of America

*Ring-Ting! I wish I were a Primrose,
A bright yellow Primrose, blowing in the Spring!*
William Allingham (1824 –1889) Ireland, from *Wishing*

*Thought is the blossom; language the bud;*
*action the fruit behind it*
Ralph Waldo Emerson (1803–1992)
United States of America

*And then my heart with pleasure fills,*
*And dances with the daffodils.*
William Wordsworth (1770–1850) England,
from *I Wandered Lonely as a Cloud*

*Happiness is to hold flowers in both hands.*
Japanese Proverb

# Flowering Quince, Apple Blossom & Daffodil

THE QUINCE is a decorative spring-flowering shrub, which Anna Christian Burke said stood for Temptation; its hard astringent fruits contain more vitamin C than do lemons. Traditionally, of course, it was the apple tree that represented Temptation, as the fruit that Eve gave to Adam. However, in the 1800s, apple blossom expressed Preference while the daffodil symbolized Regard. Only Henry Phillips, whose attributions were often eccentric, suggested that the daffodil meant Deceitful Hope.

## FLOWERING QUINCE

Latin name: *Chaenomeles speciosa*
Meaning: Temptation
Habitat: Mixed orchards, preferably long warm summers to better ripen fruit
Colours: Scarlet blossom

**Fun Facts**

The quince was a ritual offering at weddings in Ancient Greece.

When a baby is born in Slavonia (Croatia), a quince tree is planted as a symbol of life, love and fertility.

## APPLE BLOSSOM

Latin name: *Malus spp*
Meaning: Better things to come, good fortune, preference
Habitat: Orchards
Colours: Pink and white blossom

**Fun Facts**

The first wild apple trees grew in the mountains of Central Asia and apple trees were perhaps the earliest trees cultivated – in Egypt, Babylon, and China. Later, in Europe, monks planted many orchards.

Apples feature in the Bible (from Adam and Eve onwards), the Code of Manu, and 4th century BC Greek works.

Today, China produces the most apples, followed by the USA, Iran, Turkey, Russia, Italy and India.

## DAFFODIL

Latin name: *Narcissus spp*
Meaning: chivalry, regard, respect, sunshine, uncertainty, unrequited love & deceit
Habitat: Grassy banks and woodland
Colours: Golden yellows and white, orange, pink, red and green

**Fun Facts**

The daffodil is a symbol of the Chinese New Year (said to bring extra wealth and good fortune) and is the Welsh national emblem worn on St David's Day (1 March).

Synonyms include Daffadown Dilly.

Ancient Greeks associated the flower with the vain youth, Narcissus, and his obsession with his reflection in a pool. They believed that the gods turned his remains into the Narcissus flower.

# Honeysuckle

HONEYSUCKLE has several meanings ascribed to it. Most contemporary writers on flower symbolism, including Robert Tyas, said that it symbolized the Bonds of Love. This seems very apt, since honeysuckle is a climbing plant that entwines itself around its support; in the wild it often grows through and over a hedge. As a garden plant it was popular for arbours and could create a secret, sweetly-scented shady bower in which courting couples could enjoy a few moments of privacy. In Shakespeare's *A Midsummer Night's Dream* honeysuckle (or woodbine, one of its other names) grows on Oberon's bank – "quite over-canopied with luscious woodbine" – and Titania tells Bottom that she will "wind thee in my arms … So doth the woodbine the sweet honeysuckle gently entwist."

Latin name: *Lonicera periclymenum*
Meanings: Devoted affection, love bonds, fidelity
Habitat: Woodland, hedgerows and scrubland
Colours: Creamy white or yellow, sometimes pink

**Fun Facts**

This plant is usually pollinated by moths or long-tongued bees attracted to its sweet nectar that perfumes the night air.

It was generally believed that honeysuckle growing around a front door brings good luck – and, in Scotland, that this will prevent a witch entering. Bringing the flowers into the house will bring money.

Those who wear honeysuckle flowers are said to be able to dream of their true love and in the 1800s young girls were told not to bringing honeysuckle into the home because it might cause dreams that were far too risqué for their sensibilities.

Honeysuckle is a Bach Flower Remedy used to counter feelings of nostalgia and homesickness.

*I sat me down to watch upon a bank*
*With ivy canopied and interwove*
*With flaunting honeysuckle.*
John Milton  (1608 –1674) England, from *Comus*

*And honeysuckle loved to crawl*
*Up the low crag and ruiníd wall.*
Walter Scott (1771–1832) Scotland,
from the epic poem *Marmion*

The daisy stars, earth's constellations be;
These grew so lowly I was forced to kneel;
Therefore I pluckt no Daisies but for thee.
Robert Burns (1759 –1796) Scotland,
from *To a Mountain Daisy*

*Be like the flower, turn your faces to the sun.*
Kahlil Gibran (1883 –1931) Lebanon and
United States of America

# Daisy

HE DAISY IS ONE of the most common and familiar of all wildflowers. Its name is a modification of "day's eye", as befits a flower that opens with the dawn, and the pinkish tint to the underside of the petals is like a reflection of the rosy skies at sunrise. For Shelley, the daisy was "The constellated flower that never sets", and many other poets and writers have compared the profusion of daisies scattered in the grass to constellations of stars. Indeed, it is an image that recurs in the verse here.

In the nineteenth-century Language of Flowers it was generally agreed that the daisy was a symbol of Innocence. As the writer Robert Tyas said, it is a child's flower. Daisies are abundant and easy to find, and are often used in children's rhymes and games. Most of us know the simple pleasure to be had from making daisy chains: slitting the stem of one flower with a fingernail, then threading the next stem through the hole, and this simple, unpretentious picture precisely captures the daisy's modest appeal.

---

Latin name: *Bellis perennis*
Meanings: Beauty, cheer, faith, I'll never tell, innocence, loyalty, purity, simplicity
Habitat: Lawn, meadow, dune-slack and riverbank
Colours: Each white, pink tipped 'petal' is an individual flower. A daisy's centre is actually many tiny yellow flowers

**Fun Facts**
The name daisy derives from 'day's eye' reflecting how the flower opens to the sun and closes at night.
Daisy is often used as a nickname for Margaret, after the French word for the oxeye daisy, *marguerite*.
Roman legion battle surgeons soaked bandages in daisy juice to wrap around sword and spear cuts as an astringent.
The daisy represents nearly 10% of all the world's flowering plants and is the second largest family of flowering plant species.

# Mock Orange & Rosebuds

THE PHILADELPHUS produces profuse sweet scent and is commonly known as mock orange but the meanings are ambiguous. The various authorities on the Language of Flowers disagreed about the plant's emblems. Robert Tyas, whose books drew heavily on myth and history for their interpretations, believed the Philadelphus represented Fraternal Affection (brotherly love). He referred to the story of one of the Ptolemiac kings of Egypt, Philadelphus, who showed great love for his brother and so became associated with this virtue. By contrast, Anna Christian Burke used the flower's common name, mock orange, and therefore took it to mean Counterfeit or Fake. This is apt because the mock orange is named for its resemblance to real orange blossom, a symbol of Fertility traditionally carried by a bride. A rosebud generally represented a young girl and the wedding imagery of this plate is reinforced by the white ribbon tied around the stems.

## MOCK ORANGE

Latin name: *Philadelphus coronarius*
Meanings: Counterfeit, deceit, memory
Habitat: Temperate gardens
Colours: White

**Fun Facts**

The mock orange was introduced to Europe from the Ottoman gardens at Istanbul's Topkapi Palace when the Holy Roman Emperor's ambassador returned from there to Vienna in 1562.

Its strong wood does not warp and so is good for making bows and arrows.

If bruised, the flowers and leaves can be foamed up into a cleansing lather but the plant is poisonous so handle with care.

## PINK ROSEBUDS

Latin name: *Rosa spp.*
Meanings: A heart innocent of love, beauty, youth and joy, confession of love
Habitat: Garden

**Fun Facts**

Ornamental roses have been cultivated for millennia, with their earliest known cultivation dating from at least 500 BC in Mediterranean regions, Persia and China.

Rose perfumes are made from a mixture of the volatile essential oils obtained by distilling the crushed rose petals with steam.

Dried rose petals are often used in potpourri or as a romantic wedding decoration.

The world is a rose; smell it and pass it to your friends.
Persian Proverb

Gather ye rosebuds while ye may,
Old Time is still a flying:
And this same flower that smiles to-day,
To-morrow will be dying.
Robert Herrick (1591–1674), England

Perfumes are the feelings of flowers.
Heinrich Heine (1797–1856), Germany,
from *The Hartz Journey*

*Life is the flower for which love is the honey.*
Victor Hugo (1802 –1885) France

*Flowers worthy of paradise.*
John Milton (1608–1674) England, from *Paradise Lost*

*The rose has thorns only for those who would gather it.*
Chinese proverb

# *Fuchsia*

HERE FUCHSIA BLOOMS cascade in an extravagant spray over sweet creamy roses. This South American (and New Zealand) flower was first discovered in 1703 by French botanist and monk, Charles Plumieron, on the Caribbean island of Hispaniola where Columbus had first landed. Its exotic colors and forms appealed greatly during the collecting fever of the 1800s. Thousands of hybrids prospered. Soon a veritable kaleidoscope of flowers was spreading all around the world, with fuchsias exhibiting both their simplest daintiest forms and their more exuberant "frilly-petticoat" versions that resemble ballerina tutus. During the late 1800s, fuchsias reached the height of their popularity – but then interest and collecting surged again in the mid-1950s.

Latin name: *Fuchsia spp.*
Meanings: Confiding love, good taste
Habitat: Garden; needs winter protection in colder climes
Colours: Deepest purple, flaming crimsons and rose; delicate blues, pale pinks and cream
**Fun Facts**
The flower was named after the renowned 16th-century German botanist, Leonhart Fuchs.
It is sometimes called lady's eardrop.
There are now over 7,000 fuchsia varieties.
Hummingbirds are attracted to these bright colored flowers and sip nectar from the tubular blossoms with their long pointed beaks.

# *Spring flowers including Dog Rose, Hawthorn & Periwinkle*

THIS DELIGHTFUL BOUQUET of spring flowers expresses Friendship, Regard and Hope – and depicts a deep-pink variety of hawthorn, not the more common white-flowered May. The hawthorn is known as the May-tree after the month in which it flowers, and as a flower of spring and early summer it generally symbolizes Hope. Traditionally, however, the hawthorn has been the focus of superstition and, to this day, some people believe that taking the blossom into a house will bring bad luck, even a death.

Also included in this bouquet are primroses, emblematic of Early Youth, periwinkles, suggesting Early Friendship, dog roses which represent Pleasure and Pain, and daffodils to convey Regard.

## DOG ROSE

Latin name: *Rosa canina*
Meanings: pleasure and pain
Habitat: Hedges, scrub, woods, roadsides, banks
Colour: Pale pink
**Fun Facts**
Dog Rose hips are used for flavouring and in rose-hip syrup.
In some languages its name means *dog nose; in* the 1700s and 1800s it was used to treat rabid dog bites.

## HAWTHORN

Latin name: *Crataegus monogyna*
Meanings: Hope
Habitat: Field surrounds, thickets & coastal plains
Colours: White flowers; occasionally pink
**Fun Facts**
Hawthorn fruits called haws are vital for wildlife in winter.
It is used to treat some cardiac conditions.

Its fruit serves to make jams, jellies, syrups & wine.
Its tight-knit branches & spines make for good stock-proof hedges.
One of the oldest known examples in Hethel churchyard (East Anglia, England) is said to be over 700 years old; one in France may be from the 200s.

## PERIWINKLE

Latin name: *Vinca major*
Meanings: Sweet memories
Habitat: Moist undergrowth, woodlands, hedgerows, riverbanks
Colours: Blues & purple
**Fun Facts**
The name derives from *vincire*, meaning *bind*, as the evergreen trailing vines were used to tie garlands.

*See also* Primroses on page 14 and Narcissus on page 16

*Just living is not enough... One must have sunshine,
freedom, and a little flower.*
Hans Christian Andersen (1805–1897) Denmark

# Rhododendron

RHODODENDRONS AND AZALEAS were introduced into European gardens in the early decades of the nineteenth century and at that time they were considered rare and exotic. They are woodland shrubs, with brightly coloured pink and mauve flowers.

Anna Christian Burke was one of the few writers to attribute a meaning to the rhododendron; she said it was a signal of Danger, conveying the warning to "Beware". In Chinese culture, the azalea is known as *siangish shu*, the "thinking of home bush" and was immortalized by Tang Dynasty poet, Tu Fu (712–770).

Latin name: *Rhododendron spp.*
Meanings: Danger, beware
Habitat: Woodland and mountains
Colours: Pink and purple
**Fun Facts**
The rhododendron is the national flower of Nepal and a state flower in Kashmir.
The azalea is a city symbol for Sao Paulo in Brazil.
A toxin in certain rhododendron or azalea species can kill grazing animals while the honey taken from bees who have collected the pollen and nectar may be poisonous or hallucinogenic; reports of this date back to those of Ancient Greek soldiers in 401 BC.

*Flowers … are the hieroglyphics of angels,*
*loved by all men for the beauty of their character,*
*though few can decipher even fragments of their meaning.*
Lydia M. Child (1802 –1880) United States of America

*And in the woods a fragrance rare*
*Of wild azaleas fills the air,*
*And richly tangled overhead*
*We see their blossoms sweet and red.*
Dora Read Goodale (1866–1953)
United States of America,
from *Spring Scatters Far and Wide*

*When chilling winter shows his icy face*
*Blooms for a world that vainly seeks delight …*
*With alabaster petals opening fair,*
*I gladly see Camellias shining bright …*
*Like Grecian marbles warmed by Phidian fire*

Honoré de Balzac (1799–1850) France,
from *The Camellia*

# Camellias

THIS BEAUTIFUL STUDY of red and white camellias is a most accomplished watercolour. The camellia has beautiful flowers that somehow seem too rich and showy for their late winter season – but no scent, and so Henry Phillips, in his *Floral Emblems* (1839), said that these flowers conveyed the message "Beauty is your only attraction".

Robert Tyas did not include the camellia in *The Sentiment of Flowers* (1842), but in other contemporary writings the red flower was said to represent Loveliness and the white Excellence. At that time it was also known as the Japan Rose; it comes from eastern and southern Asia and is commonly found in India, China, Indonesia, Korea and Japan (it is very popular in Japanese gardens). It was named after a Jesuit botanist George Joseph Kamel. The leaves of *Camellia sinensis* are used in traditional Chinese medicines to ease asthma and coronary artery problems while seeds of *Camellia oleifera* serve to extract "tea oil" for seasoning and cooking.

Latin name: *Camellia japonica*
Meanings: Admiration, good luck, gratitude, loveliness, perfection & excellence, understanding
Habitat: Woodland; gardens
Colours: Red, pink and white
**Fun Facts**
The tea plant is a camellia.
*The Lady of the Camellias* is an 1848 novel by Alexandre Dumas; it inspired the Verdi opera, *La Traviata*.
This is Alabama's state flower.
Coco Chanel used camellia buds as an iconic symbol for her fashion house.

# Roses

ROSES AND ROSEBUDS: here the central bouquet of this charmingly informal group includes both the wild dog rose (*Rosa canina*) and the deep-pink *Rosa gallica* framed by lightly sketched rose leaves and twining, thorny stems. The rose is one of the oldest cultivated plants and the national flower of England.

In the 1800s Language of Flowers many varieties and colours were distinguished, each being given a slightly different meaning. Lovely blooms with sharp thorns have obvious parallels with love, where hurt and disappointment coexist with deep attachment. The rose belongs to Venus, goddess of love, and is associated with Love and Beauty.

Latin name: *Rosa gallica*
Meanings: True love, pure and beautiful
Habitat: Gardens
Colours: Deep pink, purple and (rarely) white
**Fun Facts**
The *Rosa gallica* is also called the Apothecary's Rose and was the basis for the Red Rose of Lancaster.
It is one of the earliest cultivated rose species, admired by Greeks, Romans and mediaeval gardeners.
Most modern European rose cultivars derived in part from this rose.
In olden times this was the only deep red rose.

See also the dog rose (*Rosa canina*) on page 26.

*There is nothing more difficult for a truly creative painter*
*than to paint a rose, because before he can do so he has*
*first to forget all the roses that were ever painted.*
Henri Matisse (1869–1954) France

*We can complain because rose bushes have thorns, or*
*rejoice because thorn bushes have roses.*
Abraham Lincoln (1809 –1865)
United States of America

# *Lilac & Laburnum*

**J**UST AS THE FLOWERS themselves are harmoniously grouped, so the emotions they represent complement each other. The Language of Flowers authorities agree that purple lilac expresses the First Emotions of Love. As Robert Tyas explained, the lilac's beautiful blooms with their rich, heady scent are short-lived and transient, like the first intense pangs of love.

Here, too, is golden laburnum hanging down in cascades, giving it a melancholy "weeping" appearance. Most writers defined its meaning as Forsaken, or Pensive Beauty.

---

## LILAC
Latin name: *Syringa vulgaris*
Meanings: First emotions of love, humility, purity, do you still love me?
Habitat: Woodland and scrub; gardens
Colours: Lilac and white
**Fun Facts**
Its hard dense wood is used for engraving, making musical instruments like reed pipes and flutes, and knife handles.
A tea can be made from the leaves, flowers and finer branches.
Lilac is associated with Easter in Greece, Cyprus and Lebanon.

## LABURNUM
Latin name: *Laburnum anagyroides*
Meanings: Forsaken, pensive beauty
Habitat: Gardens and parks; originally Himalayan valleys
Colour: Golden yellow
**Fun Facts**
It is often called the golden chain tree.
The seeds resemble peas in pods but are highly poisonous.
Traditionally used for cabinet-making, inlay, and musical instruments – including recorders, flutes and bagpipes.

For Mock Orange, also depicted here, *see* pages 22-23.

*I am thinking of the lilac-trees,*
*That shook their purple plumes,*
*And when the sash was open,*
*Shed fragrance through the room.*
Anna S. Stephens (1813–1886)
United States of America, from *The Old Apple-Tree*

*O were my Love yon lilac fair,*
*Wi' purple blossoms to the spring,*
*And I a bird to shelter there,*
*When wearied on my little wing*
Robert Burns (1759–1796) Scotland

Geranium boasts
Her crimson honours, and the spangled beau,
Ficoides, glitters bright the winter long.
William Cowper (1731–1800) England

If every tiny flower wanted to be a rose,
spring would lose its loveliness.
Saint Thérèse of Lisieux (1873 –1897) France

# A Summer Bouquet

**M**IXED EMOTIONS are suggested by this elegantly composed bouquet of scarlet geranium, gentian, and heliotrope, framed by canary creeper, wild oats, ferns and grasses. For the writer Robert Tyas, the scarlet geranium was an emblem of Folly, though in other sources it was said to represent Stupidity or Comforting. The delicate mauve flowers of the heliotrope were thought to express Devotion, while the bright blue gentian declares, "You are unjust". Fern fronds represent Fascination, grasses mean Utility or Usefulness – and the "sowing of wild oats" has long been a metaphor for youthful promiscuity.

## GERANIUM

Latin name: *Pelargonium spp.*

Meanings: Folly, stupidity, comfort, gentility

Habitat: frost-free winters

Colours: Scarlet here but can be white and various pinks and reds

**Fun Facts**

Geraniums are called cranesbills and pelargonium storksbills, after their seedhead shape.

They originated in Southern Africa.

They are much used in the perfume industry.

## HELIOTROPE

Latin name: *Heliotropium spp.*

Meanings: Devotion

Habitat: Cottage garden

Colours: Blues; purple & mauve

**Fun Facts**

The word heliotrope means "to move with the sun".

The flower is also called *turnsole*; it moves its flowers and leaves with the sun by day and, at night, moves to face eastward, ready for sunrise.

Butterflies (and caterpillars!) love heliotrope.

The sap has been used as a food colorant.

It is a perfume ingredient.

## GENTIAN

Latin name: *Gentian spp.*

Meanings: You are unjust; sweet be thy dreams

Habitat: Alpine mountainsides

Colours: Usually deep and azure blue (some white, yellow and red)

**Fun Facts**

The flower is named after Gentius (ruled 181–168 BC), the last king of Illyria in the Balkan states.

It is used to make liqueurs, beers, tonics and Polish vodka.

The alpine varieties are best known but gentians occur on all continents except the Antarctic – in deserts, savannas, prairies, rainforests, temperate woodlands and tundra.

# *April showers bring forth May flowers*

THIS SWEET BOUQUET of mixed blossoms includes the delicate white-flowered star of Bethlehem and vibrant polyanthus, set amid the pink hues of flowering currant and nodding heads of dog's-tooth violet (so named for the shape of its root). The nosegay of spring-flowering plants brings together some of the treasured joys that flourish when early gentle warmth stirs our gardens back to life.

## STAR OF BETHLEHEM

Latin name: *Ornithogalum umbellatum*

Meanings: Purity, hope

Habitat: Grassy meadows, sunny or semi-shaded banks by streams

Colour: White

**Fun Facts**

This winter/spring bulb belongs to the lily family.

Both foliage and bulbs contain toxic alkaloids that can poison livestock but not necessarily humans.

Its name *Ornithogalum* translates from the Greek as "bird's milk".

The Star of Bethlehem name may date from the Crusades. The bulbs were sometimes used as emergency rations during pilgrimages to the Holy Land and were probably brought home as souvenirs.

## POLYANTHUS

Latin name: *Primula x polyantha*

Meanings: Diffidence

Habitat: Rock gardens and stony soils but also boggy areas

Colours: Multiple

**Fun Facts**

The "prime" in primal means "first" and refers to their early appearance.

A primrose has one flower on a stalk; a polyanthus has many.

Half the primula species are native to the Himalayas.

*The daisy, primrose, violet darkly blue,*
*And polyanthus of unnumberid dyes*
James Thomson (1700–1748) Scotland
from *The Four Seasons: Spring*

*Flowers are restful to look at. They have neither*
*emotions nor conflicts.*
Sigmund Freud (1856–1939) Austria

White bud! that in meek beauty dost lean
Thy cloistered cheek as pale as moonlight snow,
Thou seem'st, beneath thy huge, high leaf of green,
An Eremite beneath his mountain's brow.
George Croly (1780–1860) Ireland,
from *The Lily of the Valley*

And like a skylit water stood,
The bluebells in the azured wood.
A. E Houseman (1859–1936) England

# Bluebells & Lily-of-the-Valley

**B**LUEBELLS signify Constancy: extraordinarily resilient, they can survive the greediest gatherings, provided the leaves are not trampled down. The sight of a wood carpeted with bluebells has often inspired poets to hyperbole; Tennyson likened them to the sky breaking through the earth.

Gloriously scented, the LILY-OF-THE-VALLEY means Humility and Return of Happiness. It has long-held associations with the Virgin Mary and was identified with the "lily of the valleys" in the Song of Solomon. In German folklore, it was said to have sprung up from Mary's tears shed at the foot of the cross. Although deadly toxic, the plant has cardiac effects and, in moderate amounts, serves as a folk remedy.

## COMMON BLUEBELL

*Latin name: Endymion nonscriptus*

Meanings: Constancy, gratitude, humility and everlasting love

Habitat: Woodlands and hedgerows

Colours: Lavender blue

### Fun Facts

In the United Kingdom it has, since 1981, been a criminal offence for landowners to pick wild common bluebells to sell – or to remove their bulbs.

It is said that if it that if you wade through a carpet of bluebells, you will disturb spells that fairies have hung on the bluebell flowers and this may bring bad luck.

They may induce a deep dreamless sleep.

## LILY-OF-THE-VALLEY

*Latin name: Convallaria majalis*

Meanings: Humility, return of happiness, sweetness, trustworthy

Habitat: Dry woodland

Colours: Usually white, pink

### Fun Facts

Called Our Lady's or Mary's tears, they are said to be a sign of Christ's second coming and a better world. They also mean Eve's tears when driven from the Garden of Eden and the blood shed by St Leonard of Noblac when fighting a dragon. They herald the feast of Ostara in German myths.

Other names include May lily, May bells, lily constancy, ladder-to-heaven, male lily, and muguet (French). In Bulgarian and Macedonian it means a "lass's tear".

Its "return of happiness" meaning derives from the tale of a lily of the valley that adored a nightingale and so did not bloom until the bird returned in May.

Traditionally, lily of the valley is sold in French streets on 1 May.

It was Yugoslavia's floral emblem and is the national flower of Finland.

*How can one help shivering with delight when one's
hot fingers close around the stem of a live flower, cool
from the shade and stiff with newborn vigor!*
Colette (1873 –1954) France

*Bread feeds the body, indeed,
but flowers also feed the soul.*
The Koran

# Pelargoniums & Nasturtiums

T HIS PRETTY POSY of garden flowers glows with soft pinks. The pelargoniums, more commonly called geraniums, were said by some writers to represent Eagerness, and nasturtiums generally stood for Patriotism. Both were favourite garden plants in the 1800s, pelargoniums being especially popular in the 1830s and 1840s, when many different varieties were grown, either as summer bedding plants or as pot plants.

## PELARGONIUM

Latin name: *Pelargonium spp.*
Meaning: Eagerness
Habitat: Summer gardens and hothouses
Colours: Pinks, mauves, reds, orange and white

**Fun Facts**

They are said to deter mosquitoes and will paralyze the Japanese beetle, an agricultural pest.

Most are native to southern Africa, but some occur naturally in Australia, East Africa, New Zealand, the Middle East and the islands of Madagascar, St. Helena, and Tristan de Cuhna.

Pelargoniums have been enjoyed on European windowsills since about 1700.

The aromas of scented-leafed pelargoniums include rose, peppermint, lemon, lime, orange, strawberry, camphor, nutmeg, spice, apricot, apple, filbert, ginger, and coconut.

## NASTURTIUM

Latin name: *Tropaeolum majus*
Meanings: Conquest, patriotism, splendour, victory in battle
Habitat: Mountainsides (often used in hanging baskets and to scramble over walls)
Colours: Reds and golds

**Fun Facts**

It originated in the South American Andes mountain range.

Both leaves and flowers have a peppery taste and are enjoyed in salads. The seeds are also edible and may be used instead of capers.

# Marsh Marigold & Germander Speedwell

THIS PRETTY WILDFLOWER collection has simple charm. The kingcup, or marsh marigold, is one of Britain's most ancient flowering plants and for centuries was an important harbinger of spring. Considered effective against evil influences, it was hung upside down in doorways to ward off witches; the sun-like golden flowers were also used as a protection against lightning.

The speedwell was mentioned in books of floral emblems and said to represent Female Fidelity. Traditionally, this roadside plant was worn by travellers as a good-luck charm against accident or delay – hence its name.

## MARSH MARIGOLD

Latin name: *Caltha palustris*
Meaning: Desire for riches
Habitat: Lakesides, swampy ground, ditches, wet woodland
Colour: Gold

**Fun Facts**

This flower is not actually a marigold at all; it is a large buttercup.

It may be one of the most ancient British native plants, surviving Ice Age glaciers to flourish in the melt waters when the ice retreated.

Pliny the Elder (23-79 A.D.) named it a plant that grows where frogs are found. Ranunculus is Latin for little frog.

Marigold is an adaptation of "Mary gold"; the flowers were used in Middle Ages church festivals devoted to the Virgin Mary. Historically, the flowers were picked on the afternoon of 30th April; before nightfall a single flower was dropped into the letterbox of each house to protect it against evil fairies.

Some early American colonists called them American cowslips and they are often still called cowslips in the USA.

Its nectar makes it an important food source for flies and bees; the flowers appear purple to bees.

The Iroquois brewed a tea from the roots as an antidote for love charms but it made them very sick.

American Colonists ate the young tender leaves as spring greens but had to boil them several times to remove their poisonous compounds.

## SPEEDWELL

Latin name: *Veronica chamaedrys*
Meaning: Female fidelity
Habitat: Roadsides, edges and turf
Colour: Bright blue

**Fun Facts**

The bright speedwell "eyes" were thought to help speed the travellers on their way.

Rabbits enjoy nibbling these.

The Pilgrims who sailed to America began their voyage from Holland on a ship called the *Speedwell*, before transferring to the *Mayflower*.

In herbal medicine, speedwell tea sometimes serves as a cough remedy or as a healing skin lotion.

And by the meadow-trenches blow
the faint sweet cuckoo-flowers;
And the wild marsh-marigold shines
like fire in swamps and hollows gray …
Alfred Lord Tennyson (1809–1892) England,
from *The May Queen*

*Flowers are love's truest language*
Park Benjamin (1809–1864) United States of America

Hope is like a harebell, trembling from its birth,
Love is like a rose, the joy of all the earth …
Harebells and sweet lilies show a thornless growth,
But the rose with all its thorns excels them both.

Christina Rossetti (1830–1894) England,
from *Hope is Like A Harebell*

Sharp gorse spines field beasts repel,
But oh that glorious heady smell!
Its scent the busy bees allure,
While from intruders well secured.

ANON

# Harebells & Gorse

BOTH HAREBELL AND GORSE are "downland" plants that thrive in dry, open grassland, fields and hedges. According to the writer Anna Christian Burke, the harebell symbolized Submission to Grief. In Scotland it is often called the Scottish Bluebell, as it is so widespread. The dainty nodding flowers attract many butterflies and bees. Gorse (often referred to by its common name, furze) has fragrant pea-like flowers in vibrant yellow – but vicious sharp spines. The fruit pod contains 2-3 small blackish seeds, generally released when the pod splits open in hot weather.

## HAREBELLS

Latin name: *Campanula rotundifolia*
Meaning: Submission to Grief
Habitat: Dry heaths and grasslands
Colour: Blue

**Fun Facts**

It was once thought that witches squeezed juices from the flower and used this to turn themselves into hares.

Harebell leaves can be eaten raw in a salad

A remedy made from the roots is said to ease earache.

A harebell wash will treat sore eyes.

Harebells may also cure depression and help to improve heart and lung complaints.

## GORSE

Latin name: *Ulex europaeus*
Meaning: Love in all seasons
Habitat: Fields and hedges
Colour: Sulphurous gold

**Fun Facts**

It readily catches fire but soon re-grows from the roots while the seeds are prompted to germinate after slight scorching.

Gorse flowers for a long period and plays host to many insects including bees. This, in turn, attracts insect-eating birds.

Ants often help to distribute gorse seeds.

Gorse has been a fodder crop, usually ground between stones to a moss-like consistency and then fed to cattle.

*Loveliest of lovely things are they*
*On earth that soonest pass away.*
*The rose that lives its little hour*
*Is prized beyond the sculptured flower.*
William Cullen Bryant (1794 –1878) United States of America

*Silently, one by one, in the infinite meadows of Heaven,*
*Blossom the lovely stars, the forget-me-nots of the angels.*
Henry Wadsworth Longfellow (1807 –1882)
United States of America, from *Evangeline*

# Rosebuds & Forget-Me-Nots

THERE ARE MANY VARIETIES of rose, and many different colours, and each was given a slightly different meaning in the nineteenth-century Language of Flowers. For Robert Tyas, rosebuds were symbolic of young girls, and there was, of course, ample literary precedent for this: poets often used the rosebud as a metaphor for youthful beauty or for transience, because the rosebud represents a moment that is short-lived. Robert Herrick expresses this in his poem *To the Virgins, to Make Much of Time*, when he says "Gather ye rosebuds while ye may." Here in this most gentle image, the delicate cream rosebuds are set among forget-me-nots that represent True Love. (*See also* pages 10-11 and 22-23.)

## CREAM ROSEBUDS

Latin name: *Rosa spp.*

Meanings: A heart that knows not love; girlhood, too young to love

Habitat: Garden

**Fun Facts**

In the early 1800s Josephine, Empress of France (and wife to Napoleon Bonaparte) oversaw the development of extensive rose breeding at her Malmaison gardens.

By 1840 a collection of over 1,000 different rose cultivars, varieties and species had been developed.

## FORGET-ME-NOTS

Latin name: *Myosotis sylvatica*

Meanings: Faithfulness, enduring true love, memories, don't forget me

Habitat: Damp places soils, near lakes and rivers and in shallow water

Colours: Blue, mauve and pink

**Fun Facts**

Legend has it that a knight, weighed down by his armour, was picking the flowers for his lady and fell into the river. He threw the posy to his loved one, shouting "Forget-me-not!" and then drowned.

# Sweet Peas

HERE THE DELICATE PINKS AND PURPLES of sweet peas are like sunset-tinted clouds. These are flowers that share the softness and transparency of watercolours.

The sweet pea has been a favourite summer garden plant since the sixteenth century. It is a relative of the edible pea but probably acquired the name "sweet" in recognition of its delicious scent. As cut flowers they look best massed together, gathered into a bouquet that includes the full range of colours. Once cut, however, the sweet pea fades quickly, and the various symbolic meanings that have been ascribed to it relate to its fragile, ephemeral character. In the 1800s some writers suggested its meaning as Departure, although for Anna Christian Burke it symbolized Delicate Pleasures.

Latin name: *Lathyrus odoratus*
Meanings: Departure (or meeting), delicate pleasures, sorry I must leave, thank you for a lovely time & goodbye
Habitat: A garden climber
Colours: Pink, salmon, red, white, cream, purple and violet

**Fun Facts**

*Lathyrus odoratus* is the original maroon-purple strain from which all sweet peas originate, derived from seed of the wild plant sent by Sicilian monk Cupani to the UK and Holland in 1699.
The sweet pea was an absolute floral sensation in the late 1800s.
Some of the first experiments in genetics at Cambridge University, England, used sweet peas.

Here are the sweet peas, on tiptoe for a flight:
With wings of gentle flush o'er delicate white,
And taper fingers catching at all things,
To bind them all about with tiny rings.
John Keats (1795-1821) England,
from *I stood Tip-toe Upon a Little Hill*

The artist is the confidant of nature, flowers carry
on dialogues with him through the graceful
bending of their stems and the harmoniously tinted
nuances of their blossoms.
Auguste Rodin (1840 –1917) France

# Holly, Mistletoe & Christmas Rose

HOLLY AND MISTLETOE, believed to offer magical protection and represent nature's regeneration, are traditionally brought indoors at Christmas. This folklore had pagan origins, but holly also symbolized Christ's crown of thorns. Mistletoe retains its ancient associations with fertility – the custom of kissing under it a faint echo of pagan times. Robert Tyas muted that holly represented Forethought because it grows spiny leaves to protect itself from grazing animals. Mistletoe (which grows on the highest branches of trees) meant "I rise above all".

## HOLLY

Latin name: *Ilex aquifolium*
Meanings: Forethought, defence, foresight, good will, am I forgotten?
Habitat: Woodland
Colours: Green leaves, red berries

**Fun Facts**

Hard holly polishes up well & is used to make chess pieces and piano keys.

Long ago people believed that holly protected them from lightning and witchcraft.

Early Romans decorated homes and hearths with holly for the Winter Solstice.

Its red berries are linked with Christ's blood.

## MISTLETOE

Latin name: *Viscum album*
Meanings: I surmount obstacles and rise above all; kiss me
Habitat: Semi-parasitic; grows over trees
Colours: Green leaves, white or yellow berries

**Fun Facts**

In Norse legends, only a mistletoe arrow could kill the god Balder.

Its Latin name means 'white sticky stuff' after its tacky berries.

Druids revered mistletoe on oak trees as the reproductive organs of Thor, god of thunder.

On 23 December (Mistletoe Day) it was ceremoniously cut.

In French villages children run, shouting, to dedicate the New Year to the Mistletoe.

Mistletoe, worn as an amulet, was said to bestow fertility and to ward off evil or witches.

## CHRISTMAS ROSE

Latin name: *Helleborus niger*
Meanings: Relieve my anxiety
Habitat: Dappled shade and mountains
Colours: white, (occasionally pink)

**Fun Facts**

One legend claimed that it sprouted in the snow from a young girl's tears; she had no gift to give baby Jesus.

Flowers were strewn on floors to drive out evil influences and ward off witches.

Witches used it in spells; and sorcerers tossed its powder to become invisible.

The mistletoe hung in the castle hall,
The holly branch shone on the old oak wall.
Thomas Haynes Bayly (1797-1839) England,
from *The Mistletoe Bough*.

The Holly and the ivy,
When they are both full grown,
Of all the trees that are in the wood,
The holly bears the crown.
TRADITIONAL CAROL

*All the woodland path is broken*
*By warm tints along the way,*
*And the low and sunny slope*
*Is alive with sudden hope*
*When there comes the silent token*
*Of an April day,—*
*Blue hepatica!*
Dora Read Goodale (1866 –1915)
United States of America from *Hepatica*.

*The flower is the poetry of reproduction. It is an*
*example of the eternal seductiveness of life.*
Jean Giraudoux (1882 –1944) France

# Crocuses & Hepatica

**T**HIS IS A DELIGHTFUL spring bouquet, as cheerful and full of hope as our first sight of the flowers themselves each year. Many nineteenth-century writers regarded the crocus as being emblematic of the Pleasures of Hope; and some, including Anna Christian Burke, offered the further meaning of Youthful Gladness.

The pretty pastel pinks and blues of the hepaticas make a declaration of Confidence. In explanation, Robert Tyas said that when the flowers appear it is a sign to the gardener that the climate is mild enough for him to sow his seeds with confidence. There are also creamy primroses here (*see* also pages 14 and 38).

## CROCUS

Latin name: *Crocus vernus*

Meanings: Pleasures of hope, youthful gladness, abuse not, cheerfulness, joy

Habitat: Dry open woods, grassy banks

Colours: Lilac, mauve, yellow and white

**Fun Facts**

Crocus cultivation was first documented in Crete; they are depicted on frescoes at Knossos and were in evidence at nearby Santorini.

Crocus corms reached western Europe in the 1560s, arriving first in the Netherands, brought back from Turkey by a Constantinople ambassador.

The expensive spice, saffron, comes from a type of crocus flower.

## HEPATICA

Latin name: *Hepatica spp.*

Meaning: Confidence

Habitat: Deeply shaded deciduous woodland, especially beech, and sunny scrub and grassland

Colours: Pink, purple, blue, or white

**Fun Facts**

They are pollinated by beetles and flies as well as bees and butterflies

Popular in Japan since the 1700s, where a range of colour patterns were developed

Its name means liverleaf; the leaves do resemble a human liver and the plant was once thought to be an effective treatment for liver disorders.

# Narcissi, Anemones & Auriculas

THE PRETTY AURICULA was a flower much favoured by gardeners in the 1800s. Here it is joined by anemones – named after Anemos, the Greek god of the winds. Ancient Greeks believed that the flowers opened only when the wind blew. Their association with being Forsaken seems to derive from another myth: as Venus wept in the forest for Adonis, anemones sprang from the ground where her tears fell. The narcissus was named after a third Greek myth character, a handsome shepherd boy who fell in love with his own reflection in a pool and drowned trying to catch this elusive spirit. The narcissus became a symbol of Egotism, or Selfishness.

## NARCISSUS

Latin name: *Narcissus spp.*

Meanings: egotism, formality, patriotism, self-love, stay as sweet as you are, uncertainty

Habitat: Woodland, grassy banks

Colours: White and gold

**Fun Facts**

In the East the narcissus is a symbol of wealth and good fortune.

Its name may derive from "narcotic" or "I grow numb" in Greek.

## ANEMONE

Latin name: *Anemone spp.*

Meanings: Forsaken, anticipation, sincerity, unfading love

Habitat: woodland and gardens; partial shade

Colours: Red, purple, lilac, white

**Fun Facts**

The anemone is used as a treatment for cramps, menstrual problems and emotional distress.

Some cultures thought it brought good luck and protection against evil (the Romans said it prevented fever) but in Egypt it meant sickness and in China, death.

The anemone is said to reappear as the swallow returns.

Folklore suggests that fairies hide inside anemones.

## AURICULA

Latin name: *Primula auricula*

Meanings: Entreat me not, womanhood, painting, importunement & avarice

Habitat: Rocky mountainsides

Colours: Many, usually with contrasting central zones

**Fun Facts**

It is also known as mountain cowslip or bear's ear (from the shape of its leaves).

The auricula first appeared in European gardens around the middle of the sixteenth century, since when its brilliant colours, and contrasting flashes and edges, have made it a popular florist "show flower".

What first inspired a bard of old to sing
Narcissus pining o'er the untainted spring?
… on the bank a lonely flower he spied,
A meek and forlorn flower, with naught of pride,
Drooping its beauty o'er the watery clearness,
To woo its own sad image into nearness:
John Keats (1795-1821) England,
from *I Stood Tip-toe Upon a Little Hill*

# Sweet Violet

THE SWEET VIOLET is so-called on account of its pleasingly seductive perfume, and is sometimes said to be the flower of Aphrodite, the Greek goddess of love. It was a favourite garden plant back in medieval times and in the 1800s. Writers often commented on its scent. In the 1500s, Sir Francis Bacon said in his essay *Of Gardens*: "That which above all yields the sweetest smell in the air is the Violet." This charming image is a beautifully observed study, although both double and single flower forms appear to be growing from the same root. Modesty is the virtue most associated with the violet: it is small, grows close to the ground, and prefers secret, semi-shaded spots.

Latin name: *Viola odorata*
Meanings: Modesty, humility, hidden virtue and beauty. I'll always be true
Habitat: Woodland and hedgerow
Colours: Purple and white; sometimes yellow
**Fun Facts**
This flower has long been used in the production of perfume.
Violet essence syrup, popular in France, is used to make violet scones and marshmallows in the United States.
Used externally, the leaves reduce swelling and soothe irritations.
As a bath additive, the crushed flowers are soothing to the skin.
In Roman times, Pliny recommended garlands of violets worn about the head to ward off headaches and dizzy spells.
The Ancient Greeks considered the violet a symbol of fertility and used it in love potions.

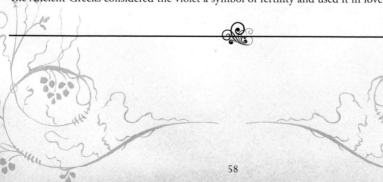

*The violets in the mountains have broken the rocks.*
Tennessee Williams (1911 –1983)
United States of America

*The splendor of the rose and the whiteness of*
*the lily do not rob the little violet of its scent*
*nor the daisy of its simple charm.*
Saint Thérèse of Lisieux (1873 –1897) France

*I know a bank where the wild thyme blows,*
*Where oxlips and the nodding violet grows*
*Quite overcanopied with luscious woodbine,*
*With sweet musk-roses and with eglantine.*
William Shakespeare (1564–1616) England,
from *A Midsummer Night's Dream*

# Azaleas

**T**HIS LOVELY illustration gathers together azaleas in a bright array of colours. Like rhododendrons, azaleas were first grown in Britain in the early nineteenth century, and in the Language of Flowers these voluptuous blooms were considered, somewhat inappropriately, to represent Temperance. The writer Henry Phillips suggested that azaleas flourish in Britain only when planted in "poor, heathy ground"; in rich soil they sicken and die, disappointing the hopes of the gardener, and so might be seen as Temperate, or Restrained, in their need for sustenance.

Azaleas are subgenera of Rhododendron, the earliest fossils of which are leaf imprints in early Tertiary age rocks (at least 50 million years old) from Alaska. All parts of the plants are poisonous, especially the leaves, and may cause an abnormal heart rate, stomach irritation and pain, convulsions, coma or even death.

Latin name: *Azalea spp.*
Meanings: Temperance, fragile, passion, take care, passion, true to the end
Habitat: Near or under trees, in acidic soil
Colours: Red, pink, lavender, purple, peach, salmon, coral, white and bicolors
**Fun Facts**
The azalea is a symbol for Sao Paulo city in Brazil and the national flower of Nepal.
In Chinese culture, the azalea is known as "thinking of home bush".
Buddhist monks first cultivated it many centuries ago.
One Chinese folktale tells how a king who had been killed turned into a cuckoo, which sang so bitterly that blood came from its bill. This dyed the April-blooming azaleas a brilliant red.

*The fair azalea bows*
*Beneath its snowy crest.*
Sarah H. Whitman (1803 –1878)
United States of America, from *She Blooms No More*

*It is not just as we take it,*
*This mystical world of ours,*
*Life's field will yield as we make it*
*A harvest of thorns or of flowers.*
Johann Wolfgang von Goethe (1749–1832) Germany

# A Bouquet of Garden Joys

THIS PRETTY BOUQUET contains several nineteenth-century garden favourites: the fuchsia, white Canterbury bells, and a purple-and-white fancy pansy, one of the larger-flowered, boldly marked varieties developed from the more modest heartsease. The pansy takes its name from the French word *pensée* – signifying thoughts, which was invariably its symbolism in the Language of Flowers – and people sent pansies to their loved ones as a token of remembrance. The campanula, with its spike of white bells, was said to represent Gratitude. Tucked in behind the flowers is a sprig of red-berried yew. Traditionally a churchyard tree, the dark, evergreen yew was an emblem of sadness and sorrow.

## PENSTEMON

Latin name: *Penstemon spp.*
Meanings: No meaning known
Habitat: Wide range from desert to forests, and alpine zones
Colours: Red and pink

**Fun Facts**

Native Americans used penstemon roots to relieve toothache.

Bumblebees love them and they provide nectar for butterflies and hummingbirds, too.

A common name for penstemon is Beard Tongue.

## CANTERBURY BELLS

Latin name: *Campanula medium*
Meanings: Distinction, faith, fascination, gratitude
Habitat: Gardens; light shade or sun; thrives in Austrian and Italian woodlands
Colours: Blues, lilacs, pink and white

**Fun Facts**

In 1597 John Gerard's herbal claimed that Canterbury bells were so named because they grew more plentifully in Canterbury than elsewhere.

During the 1500s and 1600s they were also called Coventry bells.

Bells were a symbol of pilgrimage and in the late 1380s Canterbury bells are mentioned in Chaucer's *Canterbury Tales*.

Canterbury bells feature in stained glass windows in the Archbishop of Canterbury's private chapel at Lambeth.

## YEW

Latin name: *Taxus baccata*
Meanings: Penitence, repentance, sadness, sorrow
Habitat: Often in churchyards
Colours: Dark green with scarlet berries

**Fun Facts**

Yew trees can reach a great age and some are said to be over 2,000 years old.

One of the world's oldest surviving wooden artifacts is a yew spearhead, found in 1911 in Essex, England, and believed to be about 450,000 years old.

*See also* Pansy on pages 10-11 and Fuchsia on pages 24-25.

This little purple pansy brings
Thoughts of the sweetest, saddest things.
Mary F. Bradley from *Heartsease*

Of vast circumference and gloom profound,
This solitary Tree! – a living thing
Produced too slowly ever to decay;
Of form and aspect too magnificent
To be destroyed ...
William Wordsworth (1770–1850) England,
from *Yew-Trees*

*Those will I raise aloft the milk-white rose,*
*With whose sweet smell the air shall be perfumed.*
William Shakespeare (1564–1616) England,
from *Henry VI, Part 2*

*Oh, my luve's like a red, red rose,*
*That's newly sprung in June;*
*Oh, my luve's like the melodie*
*That's sweetly played in tune.*
Robert Burns (1759 –1796) Scotland

# Red & White Roses with Bindweed

ROSES HAVE ALWAYS BEEN the emblems and ambassadors of love, but 1800s writers on the Language of Flowers differentiated between the many colours and varieties, and gave specific meanings to each. The red rose was the quintessential symbol of Love, just as it is today, while the white rose represented Spiritual Love and Purity. The fragile flowers of the bindweed (also known as convolvulus because of its twisting, convoluted stems) stood for Uncertainty.

## ROSE

Latin name: *Rosa spp.*

Meanings: Red rose – true love; (deep red) bashful shame

Meanings: White rose – eternal love, innocence, purity, reverence and humility, secrecy, silence, wistfulness

**Fun Facts**

During the Wars of the Roses in England (1455 to 1487) the House of Lancaster battled with the House of York kings. A red rose stood for Lancaster and a white rose represented the York line. The eventual outcome was a united kingdom with the symbolic Tudor rose a combination of the two colours.

Among the famous fairy stories by German writers, the Brothers Grimm, is the enchanting story of Snow-White and Rose-Red.

## BINDWEED

Latin name: *Calystegia sepium*

Meanings: Bonds, uncertainty, insinuation

Habitat: Scrambles over trees and walls

Colours: White (some pink and blue varieties)

**Fun Facts**

The seeds cam remain viable for 30 years.

It is also called Bugle Vine, or Heavenly Trumpets.

*WATER LILIES??*
*I perhaps owe having become a painter to flowers.*
Claude Monet (1840 –1926) France

*Water surrounds the lotus flower,*
*but does not wet its petals.*
Buddha (Hindu Prince Gautama Siddharta)
(563-483 B.C.) Lumbini, Nepal

# Water Lilies

THE WATER LILY has been granted very different meanings by the various authorities on the 1800s Language of Flowers. For Anna Christian Burke it symbolized Purity of Heart, but for Robert Tyas it represented Eloquence. The source of this association is Egyptian mythology. Tyas explains that the Ancient Egyptians dedicated the water lily to the sun, the god of Eloquence, because the lily flower closes at sunset and sinks under the surface of the water, then rises and opens again at dawn. In fact the sacred lotus is not a water-lily at all, but belongs to another family; it is a *Nelumbo*.

*Nymphaea* sp. first arrived in the large estates and botanic gardens of England in 1786 and was soon introduced into America, too, via Seattle's Alaska Pacific Yukon Exposition in the late 1800s. Many animals – including deer, porcupine, beaver, moose and muskrat – eat water lily leaves and roots while waterfowl enjoy the seeds. The lily's great spreading leaves also provide excellent cover for largemouth fish such as bass and sunfish, as well as frogs and, in ornamental ponds, goldfish and other carp.

Latin name: *Nymphaea alba*
Meanings: Purity of heart, eloquence
Habitat: Ponds and lakes
Colours: White, gold and pink

**Fun Facts**

Water lilies fascinated artist Claude Monet and he created 250 oil paintings of them.

Their scientific name *Nymphaea* derives from the Greek word nymph, meaning a magical female water sprite.

It has been claimed that the seed of a water lily seed can survive and be planted for up to 2,000 years.

Early water lilies were huge; fossils show lily pads were up to four feet (1.2 metres) wide.

# Passionflower with Fuchsias

ASSIONFLOWERS HAVE long represented the Christian faith. Indeed, their name refers to Christ's Passion, with the flower structure said to resemble all the elements of the crucifixion: a crown of thorns, the scourge, the sponge, the nails and the five wounds of Christ. In the 1600s, Spanish priests in South America called it "La Flor de las cinco Llagas" (the flower with the five wounds) and described its various flower parts; these were interpreted from drawings and dried plants by Giacomo Bosio, a churchman and historian in Rome – in 1609.

The American passionflower had reached Europe in the seventeenth century, but the fuchsia was not introduced into English gardens until the 1800s. Three different varieties of these elegant pendant flowers are illustrated here. Their harmony, beauty and graceful flowers represented Taste.

Latin name: *Passiflora caerulea, spp.*
Meanings: Taste, devotion, faith, religious fervour
Habitat: Worldwide except Africa and Antarctica; often in shady woodlands
Colours: Purple, blue and white
**Fun Facts**
It takes a big bee to pollinate this complicated flower and so in some regions, wooden beams are placed in the vicinity to encourage carpenter bees to nest nearby.
   They may also be pollinated by humming birds or bats.
In Israel they are known are known as the "clock-flower", after their shape
There are over 530 passionflower species.
The leaves make a soothing tea – and have also been smoked.

For Fuchsia *see also* pages 24 and 62.

*The Amen! Of Nature is always a flower.*
Oliver Wendell Holmes (1809-1894) United States of
America

*I know a flower of beauty rare,*
*Ah, how I hold it dear!*
*To seek it I would fain repair,*
*Were I not prison'd here.*
Johann Wolfgang von Goethe (1749–1832) Germany,
from *The Beauteous Flower*

# Maidenhair Fern, Orchid & Monkey Flower

FERNS SUCH AS MAIDENHAIR – often grown indoors in glass containers – were 1800s favourites, as were tropical orchids, and avidly collected. Some female botanical illustrators specialized in orchid studies, among them Miss S. A. Drake and Augusta Withers. Anna Christian Burke gave Fascination as the fern's meaning, but did not distinguish between species. Charlotte de la Tour asserted that maidenhair represented Discretion. Robert Tyas gave this a rather fanciful explanation, saying "This pretty fern conceals from botanists the secret processes in its flowering and seeding", thus embodying the virtues of discretion.

## MAIDENHAIR FERN
Latin name: *Adiantum capillus-veneris*
Meanings: Fascination, discretion, secret love
Habitat: Rainforest, woodlands, most spring edges, shaded gardens and glasshouses
Colours: Green

**Fun Facts**
The name derives from the Greek Adiantos meaning "unwetted" as the leaves repel water.
The fern was the main ingredient of a popular cough syrup called Capillaire.
It was a laxative & stimulant; it treated dandruff, baldness, coughs, bronchitis, worms, parasites, snake bites, bee stings, headaches & chest pains. It induced abortions – & maternal milk flow.

## ORCHID
Latin name: *Orchidaceae*
Meanings: love; refined beauty
Habitat: Almost all bar glaciers
Colours: Multiple

**Fun Facts**
This is a vast family with some 21,950 to 26,049 species, more than twice the number of bird species, and quadrupling the mammal species tally.
Greek *órkhis* means testicle, after its root shape: Orchis, son of a satyr, drunk at a forest festival, tried to rape a priestess. He was torn apart by Bacchanalians but was then changed into a flower.

## MONKEY FLOWER
Latin name: *Mimulus spp.*
Meanings: no meaning' but implies mimicry
Habitat: Moist soils; shallow water
Colours: Mainly yellow, red and pink

**Fun Facts**
They are called musk flowers, after their aromatic scent.
They are also called monkey flowers: many have flowers shaped like (or "painted" like) a monkey's face. The Latin name means mimic actor or imitator.

*Flowers of all heavens, and lovelier than their names.*
Alfred Lord Tennyson (1809–1892) England,
from *The Princess*

*Full many a flower is born to blush unseen.*
James Joyce (1882–1941) Ireland,
from *Ulysses*

*And because the breath of flowers is far sweeter in the*
*air than in the land. . . therefore nothing is more fit*
*for that delight than to know what be the flowers and*
*plants that do best perfume the air.*
Francis Bacon (1561–1626) England,
from *Essays: Of Gardens*

*Flowers are the music of the ground*
*From earth's lips spoken without sound.*
Edwin Curran (born 1892) United States of America,
from *Flowers*

# *Begonias, Carnation & Periwinkle*

HESE ARE SUMMER-FLOWERING plants: the blue periwinkle represents Early Friendship and also Pleasing Remembrances – and yet these happy emotions are overshadowed by Dark Thoughts (represented by the begonias) while the red carnation is shorthand for "Alas for my poor heart". Thus this pretty bouquet, albeit full of summer promise, also hints at past pleasures and youthful friendships being clouded by disappointment and possibly a hint of jealousy, too.

## BEGONIA

Latin name: *Begonia spp.*

Meanings: Dark thoughts, a fanciful nature, beware

Habitat: Subtropical moist forest understorey

Colours: White, pink, scarlet or yellow

**Fun Facts**

They were named to honour Michel Bégon, a former governor of French Haiti.

It is often called the wax begonia after its thick and waxy leaves which help minimize water loss in hot weather.

For periwinkle see *also* page 26.

## CARNATION

Latin name: *Dianthus caryophyllus*

Meanings: Red –Alas for my poor heart, admiration, heartache; Yellow – disappointment, disdain, rejection

Habitat: Gardens (native to Eurasia)

Colours include: Red, pink, white and yellow

**Fun Facts**

Carnations were first said to appear as the Virgin Mary saw her son Jesus carrying the Cross; carnations sprang up where her tears fell.

Their formal name, *dianthus*, comes from Greek for heavenly flower or Jove's Flower.

Carnations were mentioned in Greek literature 2,000 years ago and appeared in Greek and Roman garlands.

In Korea, red and pink carnations are used for showing love and gratitude to mothers and fathers on Parents Day.

The flowers have a lovely clove-like scent.

# Field Bindweed, Nasturtium, & Scarlet Pimpernel

THIS IMAGE combines wild and cultivated flowers. The pale-pink field bindweed trumpet and the tiny scarlet pimpernel blossoms are pleasingly entwined with showier garden flowers, including pendant fuchsia blooms and orange-gold nasturtiums. The message is as mixed as the bouquet – convolvulus represents Uncertainty, nasturtiums Patriotism, the fuchsia Taste and Confiding Love, while scarlet pimpernels imply a Rendezvous.

## BINDWEED

Latin name: *Convolvulus arvensis*

Meaning: uncertainty, bonds; pink ones mean worth sustained by wise tender affection

Habitat: Scrambles over trees and walls

Colours: White and pink-flushed

**Fun Facts**

Common names are withy wind (in basket-making), morning glory & possession vine.

In a Brothers Grimm tale it was used by the Virgin Mary as a wine vessel and is still called Our Lady's Little Glass.

## NASTURTIUM

Latin name: *Tropaeolum majus*

Meaning: conquest, patriotism, splendor, victory in battle

Habitat: Garden

Colours: Reds, gold, pink & cream

**Fun Facts**

Its name means a twister or tweaker of noses, probably because of its peppery taste.

All parts are edible including its flowers, caper-like seeds, and peppery leaves.

Renaissance botanists named it after watercress that has a similar taste.

The first nasturtiums to reach Europe came from Peru, via Spanish conquistadors in the late 1500s.

Incas used nasturtiums both as a salad vegetable and medicinal herb.

## SCARLET PIMPERNEL

Latin name: *Anagallis arvensis*

Meaning: Assignation change

Habitat: Roadsides and waste ground

Colours: Red, orange or blue

**Fun Facts**

The flower is also known as red pimpernel, red chickweed, poor man's barometer, poor man's weather-glass, shepherd's weather glass & shepherd's clock.

It was the emblem chosen by Baroness Orczy for her fictional French Revolution rescuer, The Scarlet Pimpernel.

Treats chest & kidney problems, constipation & wounds.

To me the meanest flower that blows can give
Thoughts that do often lie too deep for tears.
William Wordsworth (1770–1850) England,
from *Intimations of Immortality*

It is the month of June,
The month of leaves and roses,
When pleasant sights salute the eyes,
And pleasant scents the noses
Nathaniel Parker Willis (1806–1867)
United States of America

# Chrysanthemums & Winter Jasmine

HERE ARE CHRYSANTHEMUMS exhibiting the three colours under which they were listed in guides to the Language of Flowers in the 1800s – red, yellow and white. The red declares, "I love", the yellow complains of Slighted Love and the white is an emblem of Truth. The yellow-flowered jasmine that peeps out behind the chrysanthemums represents Grace and Elegance.

## CHRYSANTHEMUM

Latin name: *Chrysanthemum spp.*

Meanings: Abundance & wealth, cheerfulness, good friend

Red – I love; yellow – slighted love; white – truth

Habitat: Gardens (originally wild in Asia)

Colours: Red, yellow and white

**Fun Facts**

The name Chrysanthemum is derived from the Greek words, *chrysos* (meaning gold) and *anthemon* (meaning flower).

It was first cultivated in China in the 15th century BC.

In Japan, a Festival of Happiness celebrates the flower and the emperor's throne was called the Chrysanthemum Throne.

Chrysanthemum tea is drunk in some parts of Asia and helps recovery from influenza.

In Chinese cuisine, chrysanthemum petals are mixed into thick snake meat soup to enhance the aroma.

In France, Italy, Spain, Hungary, Croatia and Poland, chrysanthemums are symbolic of death and appear at funerals and graves.

In many places in the United States of America, white chrysanthemums represent honesty.

## WINTER JASMINE

Latin name: *Jasminum nudiflorum*

Meaning: Amiability, cheerful, graceful, wealth

Habitat: Garden (originally woodland, scrub & rocky places in China)

Colour: Bright yellow

**Fun Facts**

The genus name is derived from *Yasameen*, which in Persian means a gift from God.

Winter jasmine was introduced from China into Europe in 1844.

The flowers appear before its leaves, (*nudiflorum* means 'naked flower').

Out in the lonely woods the jasmine burns
Its fragrant lamps, and turns
Into a royal court with green festoons
The banks of dark lagoons.
Henry Timrod (1828–1867), United States of America,
from *Spring*

*Autumn is a second spring where every leaf is a flower.*
Albert Camus (1913-1960) France

*We must not hope to be mowers*
*And to gather the ripe gold ears,*
*Unless we have first been sowers*
*And water the furrows with tears.*
*It is not just as we take it,*
*This mystical world of ours,*
*Life's field will yield as we make it*
*A harvest of thorns or of flowers.*
Johann Wolfgang von Goethe (1749–1832) Germany

# Late Summer Extravaganza

A MIX OF LATE summer flowers makes a vivid autumnal bouquet. The larkspur represents Lightness and the mallow Mildness but the marigolds mean Grief while cypress is a traditional symbol of Mourning – and combining marigold and cypress signifies Despair. Here too are the Chilean glory flower that means glorious beauty, asparagus, hawthorn, rosehips, cypress and bellflowers.

## FRENCH MARIGOLD

Latin name: *Tagetes patula*

Meaning: Grief

Habitat: Ornamental gardens and pine-oak forests (especially in Mexico)

Colours: Reds and yellows

**Fun Facts**

Its yellow dye is used on textiles.

Liquid concentrate from the flower and leaves is said to stop nasal bleeding.

The plant in flower is distilled for its essential oil to be used in perfumery.

## LARKSPUR

Latin name: *Consolida spp.*

Meaning: Lightness or Levity

Habitat: Roadsides and disturbed areas; grows wild in cornfields

Colours: Violet, blue, pink and mauve

**Fun Facts**

Long-tongued bees, especially bumblebees, pollinate the flowers.

Tall larkspur is a significant cause of cattle poisoning in the western United States.

Some say the blooms look like a bird's claw – hence the name.

For information on Bellflowers *see page 96*

## MICHAELMAS DAISIES

Latin name: *Aster amellus*

Meaning: Afterthought, farewell

Habitat: Rocky slopes; sub-alpine meadows

Colours: Blues, pinks and mauves

**Fun Facts**

The name aster comes from the Greek language and means 'star-shaped flower'.

Michaelmas Day (celebrating the Archangel Michael) has been celebrated on various dates from 29 September to 11 October.

## MALLOW

Latin name: *Malva spp*

Meaning: Mildness, consumed by love

Habitat: Fields and hedgerows

Colours: Pinks and purples

**Fun Facts**

Its seeds are shaped like cheese wheels.

The flowers used to be spread on doorways and woven into garlands for May Day.

It was used in teas in China more than 5,000 years ago.

Greek and Roman physicians used its soothing qualities as a 'remedy of all illnesses' and it remained a 'cure-all' throughout the Middle Ages.

# Poppies

HERE WE SEE four different varieties of garden poppy, including two fancy "laced" kinds with their coloured petals edged in white. In the 1800s Language of Flowers their meaning varied according to colour – the red flower represented Consolation while the white was an emblem of Sleep – traditionally attached to *Papaver somniferum*, the opium poppy, from which opium is extracted.

Latin name: *Papaver spp.*

Meaning: Eternal sleep, imagination, oblivion

    Corn poppy means consolation

    Red – pleasure; scarlet – fantastic extravagance

Habitat: Fields and disturbed ground

Colour: Wild ones are red; garden poppies include scarlet, pink, purple and white

**Fun Facts**

Poppies were cultivated in Mesopotamia some 7,000 years ago.

People long ago believed there would more bountiful crops if corn poppies grew in the field, too.

Poppies were found in Egyptian tombs and a poppy goddess was worshipped by the Minoans in Crete.

Opium poppies contain narcotic drugs including morphine and codeine.

They have long been recognised as symbols of fertility and death.

Poppy seeds can lie dormant for over 80 years before germinating, this often triggered by soil disturbance such as on a battlefield.

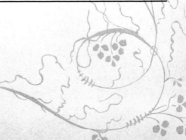

*And far and wide, in a scarlet tide,*
*The poppy's bonfire spread.*
Bayard Taylor (1825 –1878) United States of America

*In Flanders fields, the poppies blow*
*Between the crosses, row on row,*
*That mark our place and in the sky*
*The larks, still bravely singing, fly*
*Scarce heard amid the guns below.*
John Alexander McCrae (1872 –1918) Canada,
from *In Flanders Fields*

# Wallflowers & Ivy

THIS IS a truly vibrant watercolour. Robert Tyas gave the wallflower meaning as Faithful in Adversity, pointing out that it blooms "in places where ruin and desolation prevail". It certainly grows readily on old walls and fallen masonry, as well as in cottage gardens. Here the flowers are set against glossy ivy leaves and tied with a trailing tendril. Ivy grows on ruins, too, and was considered to be an emblem of Friendship, Fidelity and Marriage. Tyas observed that in Ancient Greece a branch of ivy would be presented to a newly-wed husband as a symbol of lifelong union. Ivy will continue growing over its original support long after this tree or wall has fallen so is the perfect metaphor for both Marriage and Fidelity in Adversity.

**WALLFLOWERS**

Latin name: *Erysimum cheiri*

Meaning: Fidelity in adversity, lasting beauty

Habitat: Cottage gardens, old walls

Colours: Yellow, orange, red, purple and pink

**Fun Facts**

Some wallflower species are endemic to tiny areas. One grows only on Teide volcano (Tenerife) and one only on Mount Etna (Sicily).

Beetles, bugs and grasshoppers eat its leaves and stalks; some weevils actually live inside the fruits, feeding on the seeds.

Mule deer, red deer and Spanish ibex eat their flowers and fruiting stalks.

Visiting bees, hoverflies, butterflies, beetles and ants help with pollination.

**IVY**

Latin name: *Hedera*

Meaning: Friendship, fidelity, marriage, affection,

Habitat: Climbs up trees, rock faces, buildings

Colour: Glossy green

**Fun Facts**

Ivy can climb some 60-100 feet (20-30 metres) up trees, rocks and walls.

Although it vanished during the Ice Age glaciation, ivy soon re-colonized large areas again once the ice retreated.

The fruit are eaten by a range of birds, including thrushes, woodpigeons and blackcaps; this helps to spread the seeds.

Common names have included bindwood and lovestone, reflecting the way ivy clings to stones and bricks.

*The wallflower, on each rifted rock,*
*From liberal blossoms shall breathe down,*
*(Gold blossoms flecked with iron brown)*
*Its fragrance . . .*
David Macbeth Moir (1798 –1851) Scotland,
from *The Birth of Flowers*

# *Flower Power*

**F**LOWERS HAVE been symbols for ideologies through every age – representing life's fragility, demise and rebirth as well as the Language of Flowers intricacies. This section explores flowers depicted by a range of artists and botanic illustrators. Here, the order reflects the changing seasons – beginning with spring.

## *Tulips*

### *Liliaceae*

**T**ULIPS GROW WILD in North Africa, Greece, Turkey, Afghanistan and Kashmir. Some flourish in France and Italian vineyards; perhaps their "ancestors" travelled west with Crusaders. The tulip inspired early Persian poets, become incredibly popular during the Turkish Ottoman Empire and was chosen as its national symbol – representing abundance and indulgence. The Empire's wealthiest period is called its Tulip Era. Eventually the bulbs reached Western Europe, possibly via an Austrian ambassador to Suleyman the Magnificent. Their name means turban-shaped, reminding us of their origins. Tulip bulbs were more valuable than gold in 1600s Holland; prices soared, markets crashed, and tulips became a form of currency.

**Fun Facts**

In the 1630s, a single Viceroy tulip bulb was exchanged for: 2 wheat loads, 4 rye loads, 4 fat oxen, 8 fat pigs, 12 fat sheep, 2 hogsheads of wine, 4 barrels of beer, 2 barrels of butter, 1,000 lbs of cheese, a bed, a suit of clothes, & a silver beaker.

The tulip "explosion" inspired The Black Tulip story by French author, Alexandre Dumas.

Today the flower is still celebrated in tulip festivals, especially in the Netherlands.

**MEANINGS**

Tulips mean perfect love, with red tulips meaning true love.

Yellow tulips mean hopeless love, cheerful thoughts and sunshine.

White tulips mean worthiness and forgiveness.

Purple tulips mean royalty.

Variegated tulips mean beautiful eyes.

*Flowers are a proud assertion that a ray of beauty
outvalues all the utilities of the world.*
Ralph Waldo Emerson (1803–1882)
United States of America

*Break open a cherry tree and there are no flowers, but
the spring breeze brings forth myriad blossoms.*
Ikkyu Sojun (1394–1481) Japan

Thou art the Iris, fair among the fairest,
Who, armed with golden rod
And winged with the celestial azure, bearest
The message of some God.
Henry Wadsworth Longfellow (1807–1882)
United States of America

In the spring a livelier iris changes on the burnished dove;
In the spring a young man's fancy lightly
turns to thoughts of love.
Lord Alfred Tennyson (1809–1892) England

# Iris

## *Iridaceae*

ALTHOUGH WE THINK first of the blue Iris, this regal flower enjoys a myriad hues and its name reflects this – deriving from the Greek for rainbow. Iris was the Greek goddess of the rainbow and messenger of the Olympian gods. It represents lost love and grief – young girls were led into the afterlife by the goddess, Iris. In ancient times the iris was "a warning to be heeded". Varieties include flag, snake's head, bearded, German, Hungarian, sweet and walking iris. All entice nectar-seeking insects into their whorled interiors and are designed to manipulate their visitors' passage to ensure pollen from one flower is deposited on the stigma of another.

The fleur-de-lis emblem is a stylized iris, used since the 1100s and an emblem of France. The white iris is native to Florence and flourished in its city walls.

**Fun Facts**

Irises help to purify water, improve resistance to certain cancers and their rhizomes are a vital element in the creation of perfumes and essential oils.

Vincent van Gogh featured the iris in several renowned paintings.

**MEANINGS**

Your friendship means so much to me
Faith, Hope, Wisdom and Valor
My compliments and promise in love.
Lost love and silent grief.
Yellow irises mean passion.
The German iris betokens flame.

# Aquilegia or Columbine

## *Ranunculaceae*

FAVOURITE HAUNTS of the sweet columbine (or Granny's bonnets) are woodland glades, coppices and meadows. High delicate blossoms sway in dappled sunlight in an array of blue, mauve and maroon hues – and bumblebees adore them. With spurred petals splayed like a claw, their delicate central whorls of petals are succeeded by crisply fluted, rattling seed-heads.

Crushed seeds in hot water were said to relieve headache and fever while the root served to treat stomach ulcers and urinary troubles – or to increase perspiration. Native Americans used the sweet flowers as a condiment with other fresh greens but the plant's seeds and roots are highly poisonous if eaten in any quantity, invoking heart palpitations that may prove fatal.

*Aquilegia* derives from the Latin word for eagle (*aquila*) while columbine comes from the Latin *columba*, a dove or pigeon. With its similarity to a jester's five-pronged cap, the flower denotes folly. It is also a symbol of innocence with its spurs thought to represent the Virgin Mary's shoes; columbine flowers were said to spring up where she trod, symbolizing her innocence. The fallen petals resemble tiny doves and are a symbol of the Holy Spirit, each petal representing one of the Holy Spirit's seven gifts.

### Fun Facts

In pantomime *Commedia dell'arte* origins, the character Columbine is a beautiful girl who catches the eye of Harlequin while in Shakespeare's *Hamlet,* a distraught Ophelia presents columbine flowers as an emblem of deceived lovers and faithlessness.
The Colorado blue columbine is the state flower of Colorado.

### MEANINGS

Purple columbines imply resolution and determination to win.
Red blooms mean "anxious and trembling".

*All the flowers of all the tomorrows are
in the seeds of today.*
Indian Proverb

*Every flower is a soul blossoming in nature.*
Gerard de Nerval (1808–1855) France

# The Foxglove
## *Digitalis purpurea*

THE FOXGLOVE MAY be called fingerhut, fairy thimbles (the blossoms were worn by fairy folk as mittens), fairy caps, fairy petticoats, witches' thimbles and Virgin Mary's Glove while in France it is known as Gant de Notre Dame. Its commonest colour is a mauve-pink but you often see white blooms in the hedgerows, too. The plant was said to keep evil at bay if grown in the garden but was considered unlucky if brought indoors.

The scientific name *digitalis* derives from the flower shape that resembles the fingers of a glove while its old English name, foxglove, comes from "folk's glove" – meaning it belonged to the fairy folk who often hid within and might make the bell-like blooms ring. Folklore claims that foxes slipped them on their paws as gloves and boots to silence their approach whilst hunting or raiding the chicken coop.

In China and Japan foxes are credited with the ability to change themselves into humans. Legends tell how men killed foxes for their bushy tails to use as charms against the devil so the foxes begged God for protection – whereupon he put bell-shaped flowers in the field to ring whenever hunters would approach.

### Fun Facts

Supposedly, if you picked a foxglove you would offend the fairies but if the fairies stole your baby, then foxglove juice would help you to win the changeling back.

The whole foxglove plant is extremely poisonous but herbalists have long used digitalis for medicinal purposes. Ancient Greeks and Romans used its juice for sprains and bruises. Medieval 'witches' supposedly grew foxgloves in their gardens to use as a potent ingredient for spells. In the 1700s scientists discovered that foxgloves stimulated the kidneys to release excess fluid and a tea brewed from the leaves was used to treat dropsy. Foxgloves are the original source of digitalis, the most valuable cardiac drug ever discovered which doctors today employ as a stimulant in heart medicine.

### MEANINGS

Insincerity
Stateliness
Youth

*Mourn, little harebells, o'er the lea;*
*Ye stately foxgloves fair to see!*
*Ye woodbines, hanging bonnilie*
*In scented bowers!*
*Ye roses on your thorny tree*
*The first o' flow'rs.*
Robert Burns (1759–1796) Scotland

# Wisteria

*Wisteria leguminocea*

ERALDING FROM the eastern USA, Japan and China, this vigorous climber can stretch upwards Jack-and-the-Beanstalk style or scramble and ooze along fences. The largest known is in California where one *Wisteria formosa* measures over 1 acre (0.40 hectare) and weighs 250 tons. Asian wisteria is shorter with smaller racemes. Chinese *Wisteria sinesis* twines in a counter-clockwise direction while its Japanese equivalent *(floribunda)* wraps itself clockwise. In all cases, their tendrils curl and grip in a spiraling motion.

Wisteria grows really fast and soon develops a thick twisted trunk but it can be up to 15 years before it presents its luscious lilac, white, or pink-mauve blooms. Once established, the plant will survive harsh conditions and there are legends of a Wisteria Maiden in a painting who falls in love and steps out of the artwork. Sadly, her love remains unrequited and she has to return into the picture, still clutching her weeping wisteria branch. Certainly the wisteria speaks of love lost but, notwithstanding rejection, also love kept faithfully.

**Fun Facts**

In Victorian times wisteria was seen as a warning against clinging devotion: love is a beautiful fruit, but obsession with it can choke as vines do.

Wisteria has been known to live up to 100 years or more, and so represents longevity and immortality. In Europe, families see its long-lived growth as marking the new generations and emulating the family line and immortality.

Its blossom has inspired Japanese dances and folk art – and is often given as a good-luck charm for marriage.

In Feng Shui, the tapered clusters of blossoms are said to represent bowing or kneeling in honour and respect.

**MEANINGS**

Wisteria means: 'I cling to thee', Welcome! And sometimes denotes Youth

Shin Buddhism regards the wisteria as a symbol of prayer and reverence; the branches and blossoms do seem to lower their heads in gentle supplication.

*Can we conceive what humanity would be*
*if it did not know the flowers?*
Maurice Maeterlinck (1862–1949) Belgium

*Flowers are happy things.*
P. G. Wodehouse (1881–1975) England

The gentle cyclamen with dewy eye
Breathes o'er her lifeless babe the parting sigh;
And, bending low to earth, with pious hands
Inhumes her dear Departed in the sands.
"Sweet Nursling! withering in thy tender hour,
"Oh, sleep," She cries, "and rise a fairer flower!"

Erasmus Darwin (1731–1802) England

# Cyclamen

*Primulaceae*

WITH ITS UPSWEPT cup-like petals and deliciously marbled leaves, the shy cyclamen is a delicate treasure. Different species bloom in varying seasons in a mix of environments with species native from Europe and the Mediterranean to Turkey, Iran and Somalia. The name derives from *kýklos* meaning circle – after its neat round tuber. The dark green leaves may be round, kidney shaped or heart shaped, with shining silver etchings. Hardy ivy-leaved cyclamen dimple woodland, shrub-land and rocky terrain. Seeming almost turned inside out, cyclamen blossoms are in a sweet palette of pinks, reds, purples and glistening white, the flowers rising straight up from their neat bed of foliage as if reaching skyward.

In Germanic Christian lore, cyclamens were known as Our Lady's Little Ladles and, with the ladle a symbol of baptism, cyclamens often marked the death of children, as described in the poem (on the facing page) by Charles Darwin's grandfather.

### Fun Facts

It was once believed that cyclamens could ward off bad winter weather, for in mild winters *C. coum* & *C. hederifolium* might bloom almost continuously.

Some species are nibbled by Gothic moth caterpillars while others are relished by pigs and referred to as sowbread (*pain de pourceau* in French, *pan porcino* in Italian and *varkensbrood* in Dutch).

Cyclamen are also called Persian violet or primrose, although they are no relative of either violet or primrose!

### MEANINGS

Cyclamen flowers denote resignation, farewell and diffidence.

# Campanula, Canterbury Bells, and other bellflowers

## Campanulaceae, Campanula medium and Endymion nonscriptus

BELL-LIKE FLOWERs are often associated with magic and enchantment. Campanula means 'little bell' and comprises an array of some 500 species from dwarf arctic and alpine varieties to tall woodland specimens towering over 2 metres (over 5 feet). All are much visited by bees and butterflies. The harebell *(campanula rotundifolia)* flourishes in grassland, heaths, dunes and cliff faces. Yorkshire's county flower, it is dedicated to the Spanish founder of the Dominicans, Saint Dominic, who served in Italy's Rome and Bologna. Field harebells are said to warn foxes of danger. Some sources claim that witches turned themselves into hares to hide among the flowers. Bluebells thrive in ancient woodlands where glades carpeted in a lilac haze of sweet-scented flowers offer spring-time joy but their nodding heavy heads also spread under hedgerows and sometimes carpet sea cliffs, where deep bracken acts as forest cover.

### Fun Facts

The Grimm fairy tale *Rapunzel* took its name from the rampion bellflower *Campanula rapunculus*.

Bluebells *(Endymion nonscriptus, see also page 40)* were said to ring to summon meetings of fairies who might cast spells on any who dared to pick or damage the flowers.

Bluebell common names include auld man's bell, fairy thimbles, jacinth, ring-o'-bells, wilde hyacint and wood bell.

### MEANINGS

Canterbury bells represent acknowledgement, fascination, love and distinction.

Red Canterbury bells mean deep romantic love and passion; Alas, how my poor heart aches for you!

Green Canterbury bells were the secret symbol of Oscar Wilde followers.

White Canterbury bells denote loneliness and sweetness, innocence, pure love, and faithfulness.

Campanula (both blue and white bellflowers) offer gratitude.

Harebells denote submission, humility and grief.

The bluebell means constancy, gratitude and everlasting love.

*Did the Harebell loose her girdle*
*To the lover Bee*
*Would the Bee the Harebell hallow*
*Much as formerly?*
Emily Dickinson (1830–1886) United States of America

*O, that lone flower recalled to me*
*My happy childhood's hours*
*When bluebells seemed like fairy gifts*
*A prize among the flowers.*
Anne Brontë (1820–1849) England

# Clover and shamrock

*Dianthus carophyllus* (pink clover) *and Trifolium repens* (white clover)

THE CLOVER FLOWER – its sweet nectar so beloved of bees and butterflies – dimples temperate meadows with its soft pink/purple hue. Some varieties do grow in high mountains in the tropics but most are happiest in gentler pastures, springing up resiliently where cows have munched the grass.

The national symbol of Ireland, the shamrock is white clover, its name deriving from the Irish word for little clover (*seamair*). Its three-leaved shape was said to have been used by Saint Patrick in his teachings to represent the Biblical Holy Trinity (Father, Son and Holy Spirit) with each entity integrated and part of the whole – but clover and shamrock had been revered long before by Welsh Celts and by the Druid priests who claimed it had mystic powers. Whereas today the shamrock is worn on Irish lapels to celebrate St Patrick's Day, in the 1800s the shamrock became a symbol of rebellion against the English and those wearing it risked being hanged.

**Fun Facts**

Clover is featured in the Canadian coat of arms.

The four-leaved clover is a symbol of good luck, said to grant wishes and to have been brought out of the Garden of Eden by Eve; its four leaves stand for faith, hope, love and luck.

In the fictional Harry Potter series the Irish National Quidditch sports team uses the shamrock as part of their emblem.

As a symbol of good luck, the shamrock clover is often included in the bouquet of an Irish bride and also in her groom's buttonhole.

**MEANINGS**

Red clover means "Industry".

White clover means "Think of me".

The four-leaved clover means "Be mine".

A shamrock denotes light-heartedness.

To make a prairie it takes a clover and one bee,
One clover, and a bee,
And revery.
The revery alone will do,
If bees are few.
Emily Dickinson (1830–1886) United States of America

*I have always tried to pluck a thistle and plant a
flower wherever I thought a flower would grow in
thought and mind.*
Abraham Lincoln (1809–1865) US president

*When on the breath of Autumn's breeze,*
*From pastures day and brown,*
*Goes floating, like an idle thought,*
*The fair, white thistle-down;*
*O, then what joy to walk at will,*
*Upon the golden harvest-hill!*
Mary Howitt (1799–1888), England
from *Corn-Fields*

# Thistle

### *Onopordum acanthium*

THE THISTLE IS A goodly group of flowering plants that all present a generous guard of sharp prickles. Often these can be all over the plant but in all cases it has a fearsome array at its leaf edges, these serving to protect it from grazing animals such as cattle. Fritillary butterflies adore thistle flower nectar, as do North American goldfinches.

The thistle is an ancient symbol for nobility of character or birth – and woe betide those who wound or provoke the plant but many a gardener who ignores such warnings knows just how soon and resiliently the plant springs back. Legends tell how invading Norsemen were sneaking up at night upon a Scottish encampment when one barefoot soldier trod upon a thistle and yelled out in agony, thus alerting the Scots to the imminent invasion and helping their cause. The thistle has been Scotland's national emblem since the 1200s and appeared on silver coins in the 1400s.

**Fun Facts**

This chivalric symbol has been adopted by many institutions; it represents Scottish Police Forces and *Encyclopaedia Brittanica* (which originated in Edinburgh).

Some claim that the Roman writer and naturalist Pliny – and his medieval followers centuries later – thought thistles could restore hair to bald heads.

Thistle has been said to cure headaches, plague, sores, canker, jaundice and vertigo.

The thistle is the favourite food of fictional donkey Eeyore in *Winnie the Pooh*.

**MEANINGS**

A common thistle means austerity.

A Scottish thistle means retaliation.

Then the wild clematis comes,
With her wealth of tangled blooms ...
Dora Read Goodale (1866–1915)
United States of America

# Clematis

*Ranunculaceae*

*CLÉMATIS* IS ANCIENT GREEK for a climbing plant and may initially have referred to a periwinkle. Early records suggest that clematis appeared in British gardens as early as 1569 but the species native to China did not arrive in Japanese gardens until the 1600s from whence they reached European gardens in the 1700s. At first, the only clematis found in English gardens was the native *vitalba* or traveller's joy, a rampant free-flowering scrambler that reaches 9-12m (30-40ft). It flourishes along riverbanks, flowering in high summer, and ranks supreme on a frosty winter's day when its fluffy cobweb-soft seed heads glitter as they loop across foliage. Virgin's bower and old man's beard are well-known varieties.

The Victorians took to clematis most enthusiastically and the pioneering nursery of Jackmans once held a list of 343 varieties until the dreaded wilt disease decimated their stock. However, the legacy of this Victorian passion lives on in many of the popular large-flowered clematis with *Jackmanii* a garden standby since 1862.

**Fun Facts**

The entire genus contains essential oils but also compounds which are irritants to both skin and mucous membranes and it can cause internal bleeding if eaten greedily. It is said to have been used by beggars to produce artificial ulcers on their limbs and thus increase sympathy levels.

Clematis is an effective treatment for migraine, nervous disorders and skin infections while fallen horses are stimulated by a concoction of its roots.

In America's wild west, both the seeds and acrid leaves of the Western white clematis, *Clematis ligusticifolia,* served as a pepper substitute for Spanish colonials and early pioneers who named it the pepper vine.

**MEANINGS**

Artifice, ingenuity and mental beauty.
Evergreen clematis denotes poverty.
Wild traveller's joy means safety and security.

# Hibiscus

## *Malvaceae*

THIS GLORIOUS SHOWY flower summons butterflies, bees and hummingbirds. Named by Greek physician and botanist, Pedanius Dioscorides (*c.*40-90 AD), it is also called shoe flower, red zinger, rose mallow, kirkaday and, in the USA, the Rose of Sharon. The red hibiscus appears in Indian art and is offered to the Hindu goddess Kali and to Lord Ganesha. As the state flower of Hawaii, red hibiscus is traditionally presented to visitors. A single flower behind the left ear of a Tahitian women marks her as eligible for marriage and eager for love; one behind the right ear means she is taken; if behind both ears, she is spoken for but would prefer not to be!

Ruby-red hibiscus tea, popular in West Africa, Egypt, Sudan, Mexico, India, Cambodia and Brazil, has a calming effect. In Jamaica and the Caribbean, this is a Christmas treat – mixed with herbs, roots, spices, cane sugar and rum. Dried hibiscus is served as a delicacy in Mexico. It can also be candied and used as a garnish – and is relished by hungry caterpillars.

**Fun Facts**

This is the national flower of South Korea and Malaysia.

Hibiscus is used to make the national drink of Senegal.

Some parts are believed to cure coughs and hair loss.

The bark fibres serve to make grass skirts – and wigs.

In the Philippines, its sticky juice is used by children to blow bubbles.

A popular natural diuretic that lowers blood pressure, it was an Ancient Egyptian medicine.

Kenaf hibiscus fibre is turned into paper, cloth and rope.

**MEANINGS**

Hibiscus, the flower of the hour, meant seizing an opportunity, consumed by love – and delicate beauty, perhaps in homage to its own fragile loveliness.

In North America hibiscus symbolizes the perfect beautiful bride.

In Hawaii it means royalty, power, respect and hospitality.

In Japan, it betokens gentleness and welcome.

Chinese identify the hibiscus with wealth and fame, or with a virgin girl.

In South Korea, it means immortality, long-lasting love and invincible warriors.

In Malaysia, it is the flower of celebration, life and courage – and appears on the currency.

What is this life if, full of care,
We have no time to stand and stare?
William Henry Davies (1871-1940) Wales,
from *Leisure, Songs of Joy*

*Give me odorous at sunrise a garden of beautiful*
*flowers where I can walk undisturbed.*
Walt Whitman  (1819–1892) United States of America

# Sunflowers

## *Helianthus annuus*

NATIVE TO THE Americas, *Helianthus* is named for the sun god Helios and for its huge, fiery sun-like blooms. Its centre of some 2,000 tiny blossoms that bees adore ultimately turns into a plethora of seeds equally beloved by birds and people. It has been cultivated in Mexico since at least 2600 BC and archaeologists have unearthed 3,000-year-old seed stores in America.

These tall flowers grow up to 3.5 metres (12 feet) high. Aztecs worshipped them, depicting the golden flowers in their temples. The first European to encounter sunflowers was Pizarro in 1500s Peru. Soon Spanish settlers and sailors brought seeds and gold images of the flower to Europe.

Each mature flower may yield 40% of its weight as oil – one of the few not prohibited during Lent; it soon became a widespread cooking ingredient. Its leaves serve as cattle feed, the stem fibres for paper production while hollow sunflower stems have acted as flotation devices inside life jackets!

**Fun Facts**

The buds swivel to face the sun and it was chosen as the Spiritualist Church emblem as seeming to "turn to the light of truth" and Spiritualist art and jewellery pieces often include sunflower motifs.

It is the state flower of Kansas, the national flower of Ukraine and one of the city flowers of Kitakyushu in Japan.

Sunflowers inspired some of Van Gogh's most famous still life paintings

International Sunflower Guerrilla Gardening Day is 1 May when people plant them, especially in neglected public places.

In 1567 it was claimed a sunflower plant in Padua had reached 12 metres (40 feet).

Sunflowers have been used in bread, medical ointments, dyes and body paints.

**MEANINGS**

The sunflower is symbolic of adoration; it means loyalty, pride and "You are splendid". It represents pure and lofty thoughts.

Tall sunflowers mean haughtiness.

Dwarf sunflowers mean adoration.

Every friend is to the other a sun, and a sunflower also.
He attracts and follows.
Jean Paul Richter (1763–1825) Germany

Keep your face to the sunshine and you cannot see the
shadow. It's what sunflowers do.
Helen Keller (1880–1968) United States of America

# *Fascinating Facts*

OVER 3,500 YEARS AGO Egyptian soldiers became the first known plant collectors in history. Pharaohs adorned their war carts with flowers before battle while the national plants became the lotus and papyrus. The Egyptians may have been the first to make durable artificial flowers. The lotus had sacred status. It may lie dormant in drought years, only to rise again when water returns – so it was seen as a symbol of eternal life and used in burial rituals.

When the Greek hero Achilles was born, his mother dipped him head-first into a bath of yarrow tea, believing it had protective qualities. Yarrow does augment healing and was used on the wounds of World War I soldiers.

In Ancient Roman times – and when plague struck in medieval days – wearing or carrying a bunch of herbs was said to ward off evil and infection.

In Hindu mythology, the major god Vishnu is often depicted standing on a lotus flower; this bloom figures in the Hindu stories of creation.

Roman Pliny the Elder, noted a similarity between swords and gladiolis and named the flower accordingly. *Gladius* is the Latin word for 'sword'.

When the Vikings invaded Scotland, they were thwarted by prickly wild thistles; the warriors' anguished shouts and hampered progress gave the Scots ample warning and time to escape. The thistle became Scotland's national flower.

In the Middle Ages, lady's mantle was said to have magic healing properties.

A fossil of perhaps the world's oldest flower was discovered in northeast China in 2002. *Archaefructus sinensis* bloomed around 125 million years ago.

When Mormon pioneers arrived in the Salt Lake Valley, they survived by eating roots of the Sego Lily – which became the state flower of Utah.

Angelica was used in Europe for hundreds of years as a cure for everything from the bubonic plague to indigestion and warding off evil spirits.

In the 1600s, tulip bulbs were worth more than precious metals – even gold.

The expensive spice saffron comes from a type of crocus.

The name loosestrife originated in medieval times when the plant was used to calm cattle pulling a plough.

A silky cloth can be made from nettle fibres. In Denmark burial shrouds made of nettle fabric date back to the Bronze Age. Europeans and Native Americans used the fibres for sailcloth, sacking, cord and fishing nets. During World War I textile shortages, nettles were used to make German uniforms.

The 1x3 metre (10x3ft) blooms of the largest flower in the world, the *titan arums*, smell of decaying flesh and are known as corpse flowers.

Rosebay willow herb roots can make a sweet flour.

Bluebell flower juice was used as a glue to bind books.

The poor used marigolds as a seasoning in cooking and they also served as a substitute for saffron to add color to cakes, butter and puddings.

Marsh marigold flower buds can be pickled as a substitute for capers.

Some plants only flower once. The agave (known as the century plant) grows a single bloom after many years and then dies. *Puya raimondii* in the Andes waits 150 years before flowering.

Chocolate comes from the cocoa bean tree whose flowers are pollinated by midges! It was held in higher esteem than gold by the Aztecs and believed to be an aphrodisiac.

Arrowroot powder is derived from *Marantha arundinacea*, native to India. It was used by indigenous people to draw out the toxins from poisoned-arrow wounds. Today it serves to thicken pies and jellies!

## CARNATIONS, CHRYSANTHEMUM AND CHERRY BLOSSOM

In Korea, a young girl places three carnations in her hair to tell her fortune. If the top flower dies first, her last years will be difficult; if the middle flower dies first, her earlier years will bring grief. If the bottom flower dies first, she will be sad all her days.

Christian legends tell how carnations first appeared as Jesus carried the Cross. The Virgin Mary shed tears and carnations sprang up where these fell.

Chrysanthemums are linked with funerals in Malta and considered unlucky.

In Japan the chrysanthemum symbolizes the sun and perfection while the cherry tree and its blossom hold particular significance. Hanami is the tradition of picnicking under trees popular since the 400s CE. From the 790s onwards, the custom spread from the elite of the Imperial Court to the Samurai and thence to all the people. Great swathes of cherry trees were planted where crowds gathered to have lunch and drink sake.

This cheerful feast continues today. Weather forecasts track the blossom as spring moves across the nation. Family and friends gather at parks, shrines and temples to enjoy the festivities that celebrate the cherry blossom beauty. The transience of the blossom makes it highly symbolic; it is celebrated in art, film, music and traditional Japanese tattoos. It also served as propaganda to inspire the "Japanese spirit". Thus falling cherry petals came to represent the sacrifice of youth and the first kamikaze suicide unit had a subsidiary called *Yamazakura* or wild cherry blossom. Some people believed that the souls of downed warriors were reincarnated in the blossoms.

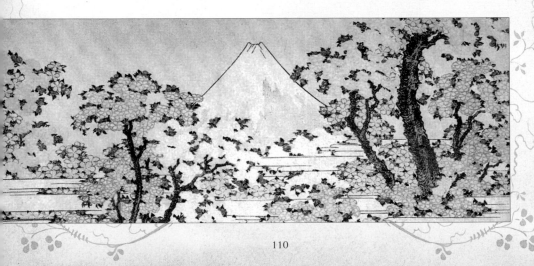

## WEDDING FLOWER TRADITIONS

In ancient Greece and Rome both bride and groom wore garlands of strong-smelling herbs and spices around their necks as symbols of love and happiness. Ancient Greeks also used flowers and plants to make a crown for the bride.

In Tudor times brides carried marigolds and ate them afterwards as an aphrodisiac! The bride carried aromatic bunches of garlic, herbs and spices to keep evil spirits away.

Germany: both the bride and groom held candles with flowers and ribbons tied to them during the ceremony.

Sweden: the bridesmaids carried little bouquets of aromatic herbs.

Austria: the brides crowned their veils with the flowers of life.

England: a little girl would lead the bride and bridesmaids to the church, sprinkling flowers along the path.

India: the groom's brother sprinkles rose petals over the bride and groom at the end of the wedding ceremony to ward off evil spirits.

By the time Queen Victoria married Prince Albert, the herbs and spices had been replaced by bouquets of fresh flowers, especially marigolds, but edible flowers were still included as well as the herb dill which was consumed by the bride, the groom, and their wedding guests during the reception; it was meant to increase sexual desire.

The posy had its heyday in Victorian times, when flowers were also the secret messengers of lovers and bridal flowers were chosen with regard to their traditional significance.

Once upon a time, bridesmaids used to prepare the garlands, bridal bouquet and boutonniere for the wedding and made posies for the guests to wear as a symbol of thanks. Roses were often chosen as they were thought to be the flower of Venus, goddess of love.

Country brides wound wildflowers into a headdress, sometimes gilding small branches of leaves and wheat and weaving these into a golden coronet.

# TRADITIONAL FLORAL SYMBOLISM ALL YEAR ROUND

Valentine's Day – 14 February: Roses (pink or red)

Mother's Day – 2nd Sunday in May in USA & Canada; 4th Sunday in Lent in UK and various dates throughout the year in other nations: pink carnations honour the Virgin Mary

St. David's Day – 1 March: Daffodil

St. Patrick's Day – 17 March: Green carnations and shamrock

Christmas – 25 December: Poinsettia (albeit native to Mexico), holly, ivy and mistletoe

## BIRTH MONTH FLOWERS

January: UK Carnation; USA Snowdrop
February: UK Violet; USA Primrose
March: UK Daffodil; USA Daffodil; others Iris (blue and gold)
April: UK Sweet pea; USA Daisy or Peony
May: UK Lily of the valley; USA Hawthorn and Lily of the Valley; others include white Madonna lilies
June: UK Rose; USA Rose
July: UK Larkspur; USA Delphinium, Larkspur and Water lily
August: UK Poppy; USA Poppy and Gladiolus
September: UK Aster (named from the Greek word for star) and Forget-me-not; USA Aster and Morning glory
October: UK Calendula; USA Calendula (and other marigolds)
November: UK Chrysanthenum; USA Chrysanthenum
December: UK Narcissus; USA Holly and Narcissus

# National Flowers

Albania: Red black-centered poppy (*Papaver rhoeas*)

Antigua: Dagger's log (*Agave Karatto Miller*)

Argentina: Ceibo (*Erythrina Crista-galli*)

Australia: Golden wattle (*Acacia Pycnantha*)

Austria: Edelweiss (*Leontopodium Alpinum*) & Gentian

Bahamas: Yellow elder or Yellow cedar (*Tecoma Stans*)

Balearic Islands: Carnation (*Dianthus Caryophyllus*)

Bangladesh: White water lily (*Nymphaea Nouchali*)

Barbados: Pride of Barbados/Dwarf poinciana/ Flower fence (*Poinciana Pulcherrima*)

Belgium: Red poppy (*Papaver rhoeas*); linked with World War I battlefields & tulip

Bermuda: Blue-eyed grass (*Sisyrinchium montanum*)

Bhutan: Blue (or Himalayan) poppy (*Meconopsis betonicifolia*) Bohemia: Thyme (*Thymus vulgaris*)

Bolivia: Lobster claw, false-bird-of-paradise (*Heliconia rostrata*) Cantuta (*Cantua buxifolia*)

Brazil: Cattleya orchid (*Cattleya labiata*)

British Columbia: Dogwood tree (*Cornus nuttalli*)

Bulgaria: Rose (*Rosa*)

Canada: Maple leaf (*Acer*)

Cayman Islands: Wild banana orchid (*Schomburgkia thomsoniana*)

Chile: Copihue/Chilean bellflower (*Lapageria rosea*)

China: Plum blossom (*Prunus mei*)

Columbia: Christmas orchid (*Cattleya trianae*)

Costa Rica: Guaria Morada/Purple orchid (*Cattleya skinneri*)

Croatia: Iris Croatica (*Hrvatska perunika*)

Cuba: White ginger lily (*Hedychium coronarium*) & Butterfly jasmine (*Mariposa*)

Cyprus: Cyprus cyclamen (*Cyclamen cyprium*) & Rose (*Rosa*)

Czech Republic: Rose (*Rosa*) & Small-leaved linden (*Tilia cordata*)

Denmark: Marguerite daisy (*Argyranthemum frutescens*) & Red clover (*Trifolium pratense*)

Ecuador: Rose (*Rosa*)

Egypt: Lotus (*Nelumbo nucifera*)

England: Tudor Rose

Estonia: Blue cornflower or Bachelor's button (*Centaurea cyanus*)

Ethiopia: Calla lily (*Zantedeschia aethiopica*); or Lily of the Nile, Easter or Arum lily

Finland: Lily-of-the-Valley (*Convallaria majalis*) & white rose

France: Iris (*Iris*) & Lily

French Polynesia: The Tiare (*Gardenia taitensis*)

Germany: Cornflower (*Centaurea cyanus*) & Knapweed

Greece: Acanthus Bear's Breech (*Acanthus mollis*) & Laurel branch

Greenland: Willow Herb (*Epilobium*)

Guatemala: White Nun Orchid or Monja Blanca (*Lycaste skinnerialba*)

Guyana: Water Lily (*Victoria regia*)

Honduras: Orchid (*Brassavola digbiana*); superceded the rose

Hong Kong: Orchid (*Bauhinia blakeana*)

Hungary: Geranium (*Geranium*) & Tulip (*Tulipa*)

Iceland: White dryas/ mountain avens (*Dryas octopetala*) and Shamrock

India: Lotus (*Nelumbo Nucipera gaertn*)

Indonesia: Melati jasmine (*Jasminum sambac*); Moon orchid (*Phalaenopsis amabilis*); Rafflesia (*Rafflesia Arnoldi Indonesia*)

Iran: Tulip (*Tulipa*) as on national flag

Iraq: Red rose (*Rosa*); originally from Persia & introduced by Alexander the Great

Ireland: Shamrock or Trefoil (*Trifolium dubium*) clover

Israel: Persian cyclamen (*Cyclamen persicum*)

Italy: Daisy (*Bellis perennis*); stylized lily

Jamaica: Roughbark lignum vitae or Wood of Life (*Guaiacum Sanctum/Guaiacum officinale*)

Japan: Imperial Chrysanthemum (*Chrysanthemum*); Cherry blossom (*Sakura*)

Jordan: Black Iris (Iris nigricans)

Kazakhstan: Lily (*Lilium*)

Kuwait: Arfaj (*Rhanterum epapposum*)

Kyrgyzstan: Shyrdak symbols and tulip (*Tulipa*)

Laos: Champa flower (*Calophyllum inophyllum*) Plumeria

Latvia: Oxeye daisy (*Leucanthemum vulgare*), Marguerite or Pipene (*Leucanthemum vulgare*)

Lebanon: Cedar of Lebanon tree (*Cedrus libani*)

Liberia: Pepper (*Aframomum melegueta*)

Libya: Pomegranate blossom (*Punica granatum*)

Lithuania: Rue or herb of grace (*Ruta graveolens*)

Luxembourg: Rose (*Rosa*)

Madagascar: Royal Poinciana (*Delonix Regia*)

Malaysia: Hibiscus (*Hibiscus*)

Maldives: Pink Rose (*Rosa*)

Malta: Maltese rock centaury (*Cheirolophus crassifolius*)

Mexico: Dahlia (*Dahlia*); Spanish found them in Mexico in 1525

Molossia, Republic of: Common sagebrush (*Artemisia tridentata*)

Netherlands, the (Holland): Tulip (*Tulipa*)

New Zealand: Kowhai (*Sophora microphylla*)

Norway: Bergfrue (*Saxifraga cotyledon*) & Røsslyng purple heather (*Calluna vulgaris*)

Philippines: Sampaguita (*Jasminum sambac*)

Poland: Corn poppy (*Papaver rhoeas*) & Pansy (*Viola*)

Portugal: Lavender (*Lavandula*) & Olive leaves (*Olea europaea*)

Puerto Rico: Puerto Rican hibiscus, or Flor de Maga (*Montezuma speciossisima*)

Romania: Dog Rose (*Rosa canina*)

Russia: Camomile (*Matricaria Recutita*); & Sunflower (*Helianthus annuus*)

Saint Helena: Calla lily (*Zantedeschia aethiopica*); & various other lilies

San Marino: Cyclamen (*Cyclamen*)

Scotland: Thistle (*Cirsium altissimum*); Scottish bluebell & harebell (*Campanula rotundifolia*); & Heather (*Calluna vulgaris*)

Serbia: Plum (*Prunus*); used to make Rakia and Slivovitz plum brandy

Seychelles: Tropicbird orchid; ivory-colored comet orchid, Angraecum (*Angraecum ebumeum*)

Sicily: Carnation (*Dianthus caryophyllus*)

Pakistan: Poet's jasmine (*Jasminum officinale*)

Panama: Dove orchid or Holy Ghost orchid (*Peristeria*)

Paraguay: Passion flower (*Passiflora caerulea*) – or maypop – & Jasmine-of-the-Paraguay

Peru: Cantuta (*Cantua buxifolia*), Inca magic flower

Tunisia: Jasmine (*Jasminium*) 2010 revolution here given its name

Turkey: Tulip (*Tulipa*); a sultan first sent tulips to Vienna in 1554

Ukraine: Sunflower (*Helianthus annuus*) blooms turns towards eastern sunrise.

UK: Tudor Rose (*Rosa*) design created for Henry VII in 1485

Uruguay: Ceibo (*Erythrina crista-galli*); also called Cockspur Coral Tree

USA: Rose (*Rosa*); chosen 1986 – native marigold also proposed

Venezuela: Cattleya orchid (*Cattleya mossiae*); called Moss' Cattley's or Flor de Mayo

Vietnam: Lotus (*Nymphaea pubescens*)

Virgin Islands: Yellow elder or Yellow trumpet (*Tecoma stans*)

Wales: Babbington or Welsh leek (*Allium ampeloprasum var babingtonii*); & Daffodil (*Narcissus amaryllidaceae*)

Yemen: Arabian coffee (*Coffea arabica*)

Zimbabwe: Flame lily (*Gloriosa rothschildiana*)

Singapore: Vanda Miss Joaquim (or Singapore) orchid (*Vanda Hookeriana x Vanda teres*)

Slovakia: Rose (*Rosa*) & small-leaved lime (*Tilia cordata*)

Slovenia: Red carnation (*Dianthus caryophyllus*)

South Africa: King protea (*Protea cynaroides*); from Cape Town area

South Korea: Rose of Sharon or Moogoonghwa (*Hibiscus syriacus*)

Spain: Red Carnation (*Dianthus caryophyllus*)

Sri Lanka: Blue lily (*Agapanthus praecox*); & Nil Mahanel water lily (*Nympheae stellata*)

Sweden: Linnea or Twin flower (*Linnea Borealis*); & European ash (*Fraxinus excelsior*)

Switzerland: Edelweiss – Alpine lion's tooth or star of the snows (*Leontopodium alpinum*)

Syria: Jasmine (*Jasminium*); unofficial national flower

Taiwan: (Republic of China) Plum blossom (*Prunus mei*)

Thailand: Ratchaphruek or Golden shower tree (*Cassia fistula*)

Trinidad & Tobago: Chaconia (*Warszewiczia coccinea*)

# Sense and Emotions

## A Dictionary of Floral Meanings

This most charming way to convey emotions, the language of flowers, is here presented in alphabetical order of the feelings to be expressed:

A flame in my heart: Red camellia

A heart innocent of love: Rosebuds

A heart that knows not love: White rosebuds

A pure heart: Water lilies

A token: Ox-eye daisy

Absent friends: Zinnia

Abundance & wealth: Chrysanthemums

Abuse not: crocus

Accommodating: Valerian

Activity: Thyme

Admiration: Camellia, Dwarf sunflower, Heather, Red carnation,

Adoration: White camellia

Affectation: Morning glory

Affection: Aloe, Marigold, Pear blossom Gillyflower, Stock

Afterthought: Michaelmas Daisies

Always lovely: Tea rose

Am I forgotten?: Holly

Ambassador of love: Persian rose

Ambition: Hollyhock

Amiability: Jasmine (especially white jasmine)

Anticipation: Anemone, Forsythia, Gooseberry

Anxious & trembling: Red columbine (aquiligea)

Apology: Yellow rose

Artifice: Acanthus, Clematis, Sweet William

Assiduous to please: Ivy sprig with tendrils

Assignation: Scarlet pimpernel

Attachment: Indian jasmine

Austerity: Common thistle

Avarice: Scarlet auricula

Baptism: Cyclamen

Bashful: Deep red rose, peony

Be mine: Four-leaf clover

Beautiful eyes: Variegated tulip

Beautiful mind: Clematis

Beauty: Calla lily, Daisy, Plum blossom; (and joy) Rosebuds; (unknown to possessor) Red daisy

Believe me: Red tulip

Benevolence: Hyacinth

Best wishes: Basil

Betrayal: Judas-tree

Better things to come: Apple blossom

Beware: Begonia, Beware, Monkshood, Rhododendron

Bewitching music: Wild oats

Boasting: Hydrangea

Bonds: Bindweed (convolvulus)

Bravery: Oak, Peony (in Japan)

Bridal favour: Ivy geranium

Bridal hope: Peach blossom

Brilliant complexion: Damask rose

Broken heart: Yellow rose

Candour: White lilac, White violet

Capricious, changeable: Purple carnation

Caress: Marigold

Change: Scarlet pimpernel

Charity: Grape vine

Chaste love: Acacia, Lotus, Orange blossom

Cheer: Daisy

Cheerful: Yellow tulip, Chrysanthemum, Crocus, Jasmine

Chivalry: Daffodils, Monkshood

Comfort: Geranium (scarlet), Pear blossom

Comforts heart: Marigold

Compassion: Elderflower

Concealed love: Acacia

Concealed merit: Coriander

Confessions of love: Moss rosebuds

Confidence: Fern, Hepatica

Confiding love: Fuchsia

Conquest: Nasturtiums

Consolation: Red corn poppy, Snowdrop, White poppy

Constancy: Blue hyacinth, Bluebells, Scarlet zinnia

Consumed by love: Mallow

Coquetry: Dandelion, Day lily

Counterfeit: Mock orange

Courage & strength: Thyme

Cruelty: Marigold, Nettle

Daily remembrance: Yellow zinnia

Daintiness: Aster

Danger: Rhododendron

Dark thoughts: Begonia

Dead hope extinguished: Major bindweed (convolvulus)

Deadly foe: Monkshood

Death: Cypress

Deceit: Mock orange, Monkshood

Deception: Snapdragon

Declaration of love: Tulip

Deep romantic love & passion: Red Canterbury bell

Defence: Holly

Deign to smile: Oak geranium

Delicate or blissful pleasures: Violet

Departure: Dandelion ball, Sweet peas

Dependence: Ivy

Desire: Orange lily or Rose

Despair: Cypress

Determination to win: Purple columbine (aquiligea)

Devoted love & affection: Carnation, Wild honeysuckle

Devotion: Heliotrope, Lavender, Passionflower

Dexterity: Sweet William

Diffidence: Cyclamen, Polyanthus:

Dignity: Dahlia, Magnolia

Dire betrayal: Yellow rose

Disappointment: Carolina syringa, Yellow carnation

Disbelief: Judas-tree

Discretion: Lemon blossom, Maidenhair fern

Disdain: Rue, Yellow carnation

Distinction: Canterbury bell

Do you still love me?: Lilac

Domestic: (happiness) Honeysuckle (industry), Flax (virtue), Sage

Don't forget me: Forget-me-nots

Dreams: Mauve carnation, White poppy

Dying love: Yellow rose

Eagerness: Pelargonium

Early friendship: Periwinkle

Early youth: Primrose

Egotism: Narcissi

Elegance: Dahlia, Yellow jasmine

Eloquence: Lotus

Enchantment: Lavender or violet rose

Endurance: Ivy

England: Red & white rose

Entertainment: Parsley

Envy: Bramble

Esteem: Sage
Estranged love: Lotus
Eternal love: Primrose, White rose
Eternal sleep: Poppy
Everlasting love: Bluebells
Excellence: Strawberry
Excitement: Red & yellow rose
Facility: Apple geranium
Fading hope: Garden anemones
Faith: Daisy, Iris, Passionflower
Faithfulness: Blue violet, Dandelion
Falsehood: Yellow lily
False riches: Sunflower
Fame: Tulip
Family union: Pink verbena
Fanciful nature: Begonia
Fantastic extravagance: Scarlet poppy
Farewell: Cyclamen, Michaelmas Daisies
Fascination: Canterbury bell, Carnation, Fern,
    Honesty, Orange or coral rose
Fate: Flax
Fecundity: Hollyhock
Female ambition: White hollyhock:
Feminine beauty (China): Cherry blossom
Festivity: Parsley
Fickle: Larkspur
Fidelity: Chinese aster, Honeysuckle Ivy,
    Lemon blossom, Plum blossom, Speedwell
Fidelity in adversity: Wallflowers
Fine art: Acanthus
First emotion of love: Purple lilac
Flame: German iris
Folly: Columbine (aquiligea), Geranium
Foresight: Holly, Strawberry
Forgiveness: White tulip
Formality: Narcissi
Forsaken: Garden anemone, Laburnum
Fragile: Azalea
Fraternal love: Syringa
Freshness: Damask rose
Friend in adversity: Snowdrop
Friendship: Acacia, Ivy, Yellow rose
Frigidity: Hydrangea

Frivolity: London pride
Fruitfulness: Hollyhock
Gaiety: Yellow lily:
Gallantry: Sweet William
Generosity: Peach blossom
Gentility: Geranium
Gentleness: Cherry blossom
Giddiness: Almond
Girlhood: White rosebuds
Glorious beauty: Chilean glory flower
Glory: Bay tree
Good education: Cherry blossom
Good fortune: Apple blossom
Good friend: Chrysanthemums
Good luck: Four-leaf clover, Gardenia, (to
    a man) Camellia, (to a woman) White
    carnation
Good news: Iris
Good taste: Dahlia, Fuchsia
Good will: Holly
Goodness: White zinnia
Grace: Pink rose
Graceful: Jasmine
Gracious lady: Snapdragon
Gratitude: Bluebells, Bouquet of roses,
    Camellia, Campanula, Canterbury bell

Gratitude & thankfulness: Dark pink rose

Grief: Aloe, Harebell, Marigold

Guileless: White verbena

Happiness: Dandelion, Red & yellow rose

Harmony (united/thinking alike): Phlox

Hatred: Basil

Haughtiness: Purple larkspur, Tall sunflower

Health & energy: Carnation

Heartache: Red carnation

Heartlessness: Hydrangea

Heart's ease: Purple pansy

Heedlessness: Almond

Helpful: Valerian

High-souled aspirations: Scarlet lily

Honesty: Honesty

Honour (in China): Peony

Hope: Almond, Hawthorn, Iris, Major bindweed (convolvulus), Snowdrop, Star of Bethlehem

Hopeless love: Yellow tulip

Hopelessness: Love-lies-bleeding

Humility: Bluebell, Broom, Lilac, Lily-of-the-Valley, Small bindweed (convolvulus)

I am bewitched: Witch hazel

I am dazzled by your charms: Ranunculus

I am your captive: Peach blossom

I can't live without you: Primrose

I cling to thee: Stitchwort (chickweed), Wisteria

I expect a meeting: Nutmeg geranium

I feel your kindness: Flax

I love: Red chrysanthemums

I miss you: Zinnia

I never trouble: Rose leaf

I prefer you: Rose geranium

I promise: White clover

I shall not answer hastily: Honeysuckle

I share your sentiments: Garden daisy

I surmount all difficulties: Mistletoe

I think of you: Pansy

I weep for you: Purple verbena

I will remain faithful: Blue violet

I will think of you: Chinese aster

Idleness: Mesembryanthemum

I'll never forget you: Pink carnation

I'll never tell: Daisy

I'll pray for you: White hyacinth

I'm really sincere: Gladiolus

I'll always be true: Blue violet

I'll remember: Tea rose

Imagination: Poppy

Immortality: Acorn

Impatience: Balsam

Importunement: Green-edged auricula

Inconstancy: Evening primrose

Indiscretion: Almond

Industry: Bumblebee orchid, Red clover

Infidelity: Yellow rose

Ingenuity: Clematis, Pencilled geranium

Ingratitude: Buttercup, Wild ranunculus

Innocence: Daisy, White carnation, White rose, White violet

Innocent & faithful: White Canterbury bell

Insincerity: Foxglove

Insinuation: Great bindweed

Instability: Dahlia

Intemperance: Grape vine

Invitation to dance: Viscaria

Jealousy: Hyacinth, Marigold, Yellow Hyacinth, Yellow rose

Joy: Crocus, Gardenia, Red & yellow rose

Joys to come: Celandine

Kindness (Japan): Cherry blossom

Kiss me: Mistletoe

Knight errant: Monkshood

Lasting affection: Magenta zinnia

Lasting beauty: Gillyflower, Stock, Wallflowers

Lasting friendship: Pear blossom

Let me go: Buttercup

Let's take a chance on happiness: White violet

Life & immortality: Acorn

Life's transience: Cherry blossom

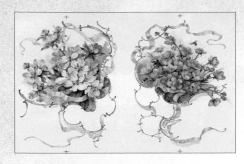

Light-heartedness: Shamrock

Lightness: Larkspur

Lofty wise thoughts: Tall sunflower

Long life: Peach or plum blossom

Longing: Pink camellia

Love: Aster, Orchid, Red rose; (at first sight) Blue rose, Gloxinia, Lavender or violet rose, Thornless rose; (bonds) Honeysuckle; (forsaken) Willow; (in absence) Myrtle; (in all seasons) Gorse; (of nature) Magnolia; Chinese aster (promise) Iris; (reciprocated) Ambrosia

Loveliness: Red camellia

Lovely: White Canterbury bell

Lowliness: Bramble

Loyalty: Daisy

Luck: Bells of Ireland

Lust: Coriander

Magic: Witch hazel, Fern

Maiden charms: Eucharis lily

Majesty: Imperial lily

Make haste: Dianthus

Malevolence: Lobelia

Marriage: Ivy, Myrtle

Masculinity: Peony

May I have the next dance?: Ivy geranium

Meeting: Sweet peas

Melancholy: Dark geranium, Lavender, Oak geranium

Memories: Forget-me-nots, Mock orange, Syringa, White lilac

Merriment: Pansy

Misanthropy: Aconite, Fuller's thistle

Mistrust: Lavender

Modesty: Blue violet, Lily, Peach rose, Sweet violet, White violet, Yellow jasmine

Moral and mental beauty: Mignonette

Mother (Chinese emblem): Day lily

Mother's love: Pink carnation

Mourning: Cypress, Dark crimson rose, Weeping willow

My compliments: Iris

My love for you can't wait: Balsam

Mystery: Blue rose

Neatness: Broom

Never: Snapdragon

Night: Blue minor bindweed (convolvulus)

No: Snapdragon

Nobility: Magnolia

Not heartless: Love-lies-bleeding

Oblivion: Poppy

Obstacles to be overcome: Mistletoe

Oscar Wilde (secret follower of): Green Canterbury bell:

Our wonderful family/household: Sage

Pain & grief: Marigold

Painting: Auricula

Participation: Double daisy

Passion: Azalea, Orange lily, Orange or coral rose, Yellow iris:

Patience: Ox-eye daisy

Patriotism: Narcissus, Nasturtium

Peace: Red corn poppy

Penitence: Yew

Pensive beauty: Laburnum

Pensiveness: Cowslip

Perfection: White camellia; (excellence) Camellia, Wild strawberry; (goodness) Strawberry; (perfect happiness) Pink rose; (perfect love) Tulip

Play: Red or pink hyacinth

Please forgive me: Purple hyacinth

Pleasure: Red poppy

Pleasure and pain: Dog rose

Poverty: Evergreen clematis

Pray for me: White verbena

Preference: Apple blossom, apple geranium
Presumption: Snapdragon
Pretty love: Marigold
Pride: Amaryllis, Magnolia
Promise: Almond
Promptness: Ten-week stock
Prosperity: Peony
Protection: White heather
Proud spirit: Gloxinia
Purity: Daisy, Lily, Lotus, White carnation,
    White lilac, White lily, White verbena,
    White violet; (& lofty thoughts)
    Sunflower; (and loveliness) Red rosebuds
Purity, reverence & humility: White rose
Radiant charm: Ranunculus
Rapture: Valerian
Rare or delicate beauty: Hibiscus
Rashness: Hyacinth
Readiness: Red valerian
Ready-armed: Gladiolus
Recall: Silver-leaf geranium
Refined beauty: Orchid
Refusal & apologies: Striped carnation
Regard: Daffodils
Regret: Purple verbena, Rue
Regrets for ever: Asphodel
Rejection: Yellow carnation
Relieve my anxiety: Christmas rose
Religious fervour:
    Passionflower
Remembrance: Rosemary
Remorse: Bramble,
    Raspberry
Rendezvous: Stitchwort
    (chickweed)
Repentance: Yew
Repose: Blue (minor)
    bindweed
Resignation: Cyclamen
Resolution: Purple
    columbine (aquiligea)
Respect: Daffodils
Retaliation: Scottish thistle

Return my affection: Jonquil
Returning happiness: Lily-of-the-Valley
Reward of virtue: Garland or wreath of roses
Riches: Buttercup
Royalty: Purple tulip
Rural happiness: Yellow violet
Rustic beauty: French honeysuckle
Sacred: Marigold
Secrecy: White rose
Secret love: Acacia
Secret & sweet love: Gardenia
Secret love bond: Maidenhair fern
Self-love: Narcissi
Sensibility: Scarlet verbena
Sensitiveness: Mimosa, Verbena
Sensuality: Spanish jasmine
Separation: Carolina jasmine
Shame: Peony
Shelter: Fern
Sickness: Field anemones
Silence: White rose
Silent love: Primrose
Silliness: Scarlet geranium
Simplicity: Daisy
Sincerity: Anemones, Honesty
Slander: Nettle
Sleep: White poppy
Slighted love: Yellow chrysanthemums
Solitude: Heather
Sorrow: Cypress, Marigold,
    Purple hyacinth, Yew
Sorry I must leave: Sweet peas
Sorry I'm not with you:
    Striped carnation
Splendour: Nasturtiums
Sports & games: Hyacinth
Stateliness: Foxglove
Stay as sweet as you are: Narcissi
Steadfast piety: Wild geranium
Strong character: Gladiolus
Strong emotion: Yellow rose
Stupidity: Nuts, Almond, Scarlet
    geranium

Submission: Grass, harebell
Success: Yellow poppy
Sunny smiles: Yellow tulip
Sunshine: Daffodils, Yellow tulip
Sweet: White Canterbury bell
Sweet & lovely: White carnation
Sweet be thy dreams: Gentian
Sweetness: Lily-of-the-Valley
Sympathy: Sweetbriar rose
Take care: Azalea
Temperance: Azalea
Temptation: Quince
Thank you for a lovely time & goodbye: Sweet peas
Thank you for understanding: Hydrangea
Thankfulness: Agrimony
Think of me: Pansy, White clover
Thrift: Thyme
Too young to love: White rosebuds
Touch me not: Red Balsam
Tranquilize my anxiety: Christmas
Transcending space & time: Delphinium
Transport of joy: Cape jasmine
Treachery: Monkshood
True: (excellence) White camellia;
    (friendship) Oak-leaf geranium; (love)
    Forget-me-nots, Red rose, Red tulip); (to
    the end) Azalea
Trust: Aster, Freesia
Trustworthy: Lily-of-the-Valley
Truth: Anemones, White chrysanthemums
Uncertainty: Bindweed (convolvulus),
    Daffodils, Narcissus
Unconscious beauty: Burgundy rose
Understanding: Camellia
Unexpected meeting: Lemon geranium
Unfading love: Anemones
Unfortunate love: Scabious
Unity: Red & white rose
Unobtrusive loveliness: White hyacinth
Unpatronized merit: Red primrose
Unrequited love & deceit: Daffodils
Uselessness: Spiraea (meadowsweet)
Vain-glory: Hydrangea

Valor: Iris
Victory in battle: Nasturtiums
Virtue: Mint
Watchfulness: Dame violet
Wealth & prosperity: Jasmine, Yellow poppy,
    Wheat
Welcome: Mayflower, Wisteria
Well-bred: Scarlet lily
Whimsical: Purple carnation
Widowhood: Scabious
Will you smile?: Sweet William
Winning grace: Cowslip
Winning the impossible: Blue rose
Wisdom: Iris
Wishes come true: White heather
Wishes for prosperity: Red-leaved rose
Wistfulness: White rose
With joy: Myrtle
Womanhood (Chinese symbol): Auricula,
    Azalea
Woman's love: Pink carnation
Worth & loveliness: Mignonette
Worth sustained by tender affection: Pink
    bindweed
Worthiness: White tulip
Yes: Solid colour carnation
You are …: (beautiful) Full-blown rose; (rich
    in attractions) Garden ranunculus; (queen
    of coquettes) Dame violet; (young and
    beautiful) Red rosebuds
You may hope: Rose leaf
You occupy my thoughts: Purple violet
You puzzle me: Love-in-a-mist
You'll always be beautiful to me: Stock
Your devout admirer: Dwarf sunflower
Your friendship means so much to me: Iris
Your purity equals your loveliness: Orange
    blossom
You're lovely: Gardenia
Youth: Foxglove, Wisteria; (youthful gladness)
    Crocus; (youthful innocence) White lilac
Zealour: Elderflower
Zest: Lemon blossom

# Index of flowers and their meanings

white: candour, memories, pure, youthful innocence
**Lily-of-the-Valley 40-41** sweetness, humility, returning happiness, trustworthy

**Maidenhair Fern 70-71** discretion, secret love bond
**Mallow 78-79** consumed by love, mildness
**Marigold 44-45** affection, caress, comforts heart, cruelty, grief, jealousy, pain & grief, pretty love, sacred, sorrow
**Marigold (French) 78-79** grief
**Marigold, Marsh 44-45** desire for riches
**Michaelmas Daisies 78-79** afterthought, farewell
**Mignonette 18-19** moral and mental beauty, qualities surpass charms, worth and loveliness
**Mistletoe 52-53** I surmount all difficulties, kiss me, obstacles to be overcome (sacred plant of the druids and of India)
**Mock Orange 22-23, 34-35** counterfeit, deceit, memory
**Monkey Flower (mimulus) 70-71** no 'language meaning'; implies mimicry

**Narcissi 56-57** egotism, formality, patriotism, self-love, stay as sweet as you are, uncertainty
**Nasturtiums 42-43, 74-75** conquest, patriotism, splendour, victory in battle

**Orchid 70-71** love; refined beauty
bumblebee orchid: industry

**Pansy 8-9, 62-63** I think of you, merriment, think of me
purple: heart's ease
**Passionflower 68-69** devotion, faith, religious fervour, taste
**Pelargonium 42-43** patriotism
**Penstemon 62-63**
**Periwinkle 26-27, 72-73** Sweet memories
**Polyanthus 38-39** diffidence
**Poppies 80-81** eternal sleep, imagination, oblivion
corn: consolation
red: pleasure

scarlet: fantastic extravagance
white: consolation, dreams, modern, peace
yellow: wealth, success
white: consolation dreams, modern, my antidote, my bane, oblivion, peace, sleep & sleeping heart
**Primrose 14-15, 26-27** early youth, eternal love, I can't live without you, modest worth, silent love
evening: inconstancy
red: unpatronized merit
**Primula 54-55** *see also* primrose

**Quince 16-17** temptation

**Rhododendrons 28-29** beware, danger
**Rosebuds 22-23, 48-49** a heart innocent of love, beauty and joy, confession of love
moss: confession of love
red: pure and lovely; you are young and beautiful
white: a heart that knows not love; girlhood, too young to love
**Rosehips 78-79**
**Roses 22-23, 32-33, 48-49, 64-65, 78-79** blue: love at first sight, mystery, winning the impossible
burgundy: unconscious beauty
crimson (dark): mourning
lavender (or violet): enchantment, love at first sight
orange or coral: desire, fascination, passion
peach: modesty
pink: grace, perfect happiness; (dark pink) gratitude & thankfulness
red: true love; (deep red) bashful shame
red & yellow: joy, happiness, excitement
red and white together: unity, emblem of England
thornless: love at first sight
white: eternal love, innocence, purity, reverence and humility, secrecy, silence, wistfulness
yellow: apology, broken heart, dire betrayal, dying love, friendship, jealousy, infidelity, strong emotion
bouquet: gratitude
Christmas: tranquilize my anxiety
damask: brilliant complexion; freshness

dog: pleasure and pain
full-blown: you are beautiful
garland or wreath: reward of virtue
leaf: I never trouble, you may hope
Persian: ambassador of love
red leaved: wishes for prosperity
sweetbriar: sympathy
tea: always lovely, I'll remember

**Scarlet Pimpernel 74-75** change, assignation
**Shamrock 98-99** *see* clover
**Snowdrop 12-13** a friend in adversity,
  consolation, hope
**Speedwell 44-45** fidelity
**Spiraea (meadowsweet) 74-75** uselessness
**Star of Bethlehem 38-39** hope, purity
**Stitchwort (chickweed) 44-45** rendezvous, I cling
  to thee
**Strawberry 14-15** excellence, foresight, perfect
  goodness
**Sunflower 106-107** false riches, pure and lofty
  thoughts
  dwarf: adoration, your devout admirer
  tall: haughtiness & pride, lofty wise
  thoughts;
**Sweet Peas 50-51** departure (or meeting), sorry
  I must leave, thank you for a lovely time &
  goodbye, delicate or blissful pleasures;
**Sweet Violet 58-59** *see* Violet

**Thistle 100-101** common thistle: austerity
  thistle, fuller's: misanthropy
  Scottish thistle: retaliation
**Tulips 84-85** declaration of love; fame, perfect love;
  emblem of Holland and Turkey
  purple: royalty
  red: true love, believe me
  variegated: beautiful eyes
  white: worthiness & forgiveness
  yellow: cheerful thoughts, hopeless love, sunshine
  & sunny smiles

**Violet 38-39, 58-59** blue: faithfulness; modesty,
  modest love; I will remain faithful; I'll always be true
  dame: watchfulness; you are the queen of
  coquettes
  purple: you occupy my thoughts
  sweet: modesty
  white: purity, candor, modesty, innocence, let's
  take a chance on happiness
  yellow: modest worth, rural happiness

**Wallflowers 82-83** fidelity in adversity, lasting beauty
**Water Lilies 66-67** a pure heart
**Wild Oats 36-37** music (witching soul of music)
**Wild Strawberry 14-15** perfect excellence
**Wisteria 92-93** I cling to thee, welcome! youth

**Yew 62-63** penitence, repentance, sadness, sorrow

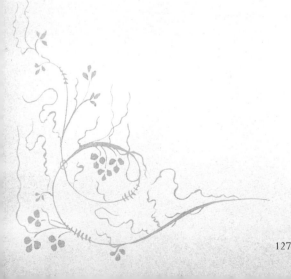

# *Acknowledgements*

This book and its introduction draws in part upon the thoughts expressed about Fanny
   Robinson's *The Book of Memory* by Gill Saunders, senior curator in the Department of Prints,
   Drawings and Paintings at the Victoria and Albert Museum, London.
The illustrations in pages 10–82 are all by Fanny Robinson.
Other illustrations are from antique sources (some found via Wikimedia Commons) while details
   of the illustrations by Fanny Robinson have been used throughout the book.

Thanks are also due to:
John Luscombe and Grant Luscombe as the recognized copyright holders of *The Book of Memory*.
Landlife, the registered charity to whom royalties from sales of the publication have been donated
   by the original copyright holders.
Cristina Galimberti for her astute editorial direction.
Peggy Vance to whom the publisher gives thanks for all the support in the creation of the book in
   which Fanny Robinson's botanical illustrations were first published, *The Country Flowers of a
   Victorian Lady* (Apollo Publishing Ltd., 1999).

The publisher wishes to apologise for any omissions, especially if a favourite bloom has not been
   featured in this book – but the lists and meanings explored here concentrate on those flowers
   actually depicted in the book.

# *Bibliography*

Robinson, Fanny: *The Country Flowers of a Victorian Lady* Apollo Publishing Ltd., 1999
Gray, Samantha: *The Secret Language of Flowers* Cico Books, London, 2011
Kirkby, Mandy: *The Language of Flowers; a Miscellany* Macmillan, London, 2011
Mabey, Richard: *Flora Brittannica* Chatto & Windus, London, 1996
Pickston, Margaret: *The Language of Flowers* Michael Joseph Ltd., London, 1968 (11th edition
   1995)
*Reader's Digest Encyclopaedia of Garden Plants and Flowers* Reader's Digest Association Ltd.,
   London, 1971
Wells, Diana: *100 Flowers and How they got their names* (Algonquin Books of Chapel Hill, a
   division of Workman Publishing) New York, 1997